LUKE: GRACIOUS THEOLOGIAN

D1634393

There is salvation in no one else,
for there is no other name under heaven
given among mortals
by which we must be saved.
(Acts 4:12)

Wilfrid J. Harrington, O.P.

Luke: Gracious Theologian
The Jesus of Luke

the columba press

First published, 1997, by
the columba press
55A Spruce Avenue, Stillorgan Industrial Park,
Blackrock, Co Dublin

Cover by Bill Bolger
Origination by The Columba Press
Printed in Ireland by Colour Books Ltd, Dublin

ISBN 1 85607 206 1

Contents

Introduction

In a recent book I introduced the Jesus discerned and presented by Mark in his gospel.[1] Here I do the same for Luke and his gospel. The central figure is the self-same Jesus but viewed through the prism of each evangelist's perception. Mark's gospel is, firmly, a *theologia crucis*, a theology of the cross. He is convinced that until one comes to terms with the cross one cannot really understand Jesus and, *a fortiori*, one cannot effectively proclaim him. This is why the climax of his gospel is the centurion's statement: 'Truly this man was God's Son' (Mk 15:39). The centurion had come to terms with the cross and could make a Christian profession of faith.

Luke, also, acknowledges the significance of the death of Jesus. His focus, however, is elsewhere. As 'image of the invisible God' (Col 1:15), Jesus displayed the graciousness of God. Luke had become keenly aware of that graciousness through his understanding of Jesus. This is why, in Luke's portrayal, he took pains to emphasise the praxis of Jesus in word and deed. For him, Jesus is Saviour – Saviour in word and deed. The Lucan Jesus displays notable and consistent concern for the marginalised. These include, surely, the poor and women. Those in direst need were sinners. Jesus was their friend. This was scandal to the righteous. Jesus would not be turned aside. He knew that the Father was a God of infinite love, therefore a God of limitless mercy and forgiveness. Jesus would be witness to his God even to death. In his portrayal Luke, uniquely, has Jesus continue his saving mission throughout his passion.

Unlike Mark – his main source – Luke has an infancy narrative (Lk 1-2). This is not only distinctive; these chapters underline the artistic creativity and theological acumen of Luke. Here, in lovely story form, he displays his christology. Before the reader gets into the story proper, one knows who this Jesus is: he is Son of David, Son of

God, Saviour, Messiah, Lord. All the while, he is a new-born babe, helpless in swaddling-cloths. Luke's Christian reader knows that the adult Jesus will end his life nailed helplessly to a cross. Luke, like Mark, had grasped what Paul had perceived long before them, that our God, precisely because he *is* God, and *our* God, displays his power in weakness (see 1 Cor 1:22-25). He is, consistently, God of forgiveness. And Jesus preached forgiveness.

Each evangelist offers a distinctive portrait of Jesus. Critical study of our gospels brings us back to the 'historical' Jesus – what we can know of the Jesus of Nazareth who lived, suffered and died in first-century Palestine. The Mark book has a short chapter which outlines the result of scholarly investigation. Reference to that text might suffice. It is thought more practical to reproduce it. Apart from that, because Luke has leaned heavily on Mark, much of the Marcan presentation is presupposed. This book and its predecessor are complementary. The emphasis, here, is firmly on the Lucan perspective.

CHAPTER 1

Luke

Only Luke is with me now (2 Tim 4:11)

Luke was a second or, perhaps, third-generation Christian. He was surely a Gentile and a native, very likely, of Syrian Antioch. He was well educated, a fact borne out by the quality and flexibility of his Greek style. He was, evidently, well versed in the Greek Bible. There is impressive traditional witness to his authorship of the third gospel and Acts of the Apostles. A Luke is mentioned three times in the New Testament: in Philemon 24, listed among Paul's fellow workers; in Col 4:14, Luke, the 'beloved physician,' and in 2 Tim 4:11, 'Only Luke is with me.' If this Luke is author of Luke-Acts, it would make him a companion of Paul. In the same line are the so-called We-Sections of Acts (16:10-17; 20:5-15; 21:1-18; 27:1-28:16) where the author writes in the first person. While it may be maintained that this is no more than a recognised Hellenistic literary convention, it is arguable that the passages are something of a diary. On the other hand, the author of Luke-Acts shows no acquaintance with Paul's letters. If we, reasonably, accept the attribution of the authorship of Luke-Acts to the named New Testament Luke, we may think of him as having been for some time an associate of Paul. He would have been unfamiliar with the earlier career of Paul – hence some discrepancies between his account of events and Paul's. And he would have written before there was a collection of Paul's letters.

It is not possible to determine where Luke-Acts was written. As to date: it was written after Mark (usually dated around 70 AD). The gospel presupposes the destruction of Jerusalem by the Romans (Lk 13:35; 21:20). The prevailing tendency is to date the whole work 80-85 AD.

It is unfortunate that an understandable desire to group the four gospels meant the separation of Acts of the Apostles from the gospel of Luke. The fact is, gospel and Acts belong together as two parts of a single work. The gospel begins in Jerusalem, more specifically in the temple, with the message of the angel to Zechariah; it closes with the disciples of Jesus at prayer in the temple (Lk 24:53). The plan of Acts is firmly sketched in Acts 1:18 – 'You will be my witnesses in Jerusalem, in all Judaea and Samaria, and to the ends of the earth.' There are few more dramatic endings in literature than the picture of Paul, in Rome (the Roman Empire, remember, is the 'world' of the New Testament) under house-arrest, 'proclaiming the kingdom of God and teaching about the Lord Jesus Christ with all boldness and without hindrance' (Acts 28:31). Jerusalem is central. In the gospel, the movement is *toward* Jerusalem; in Acts the movement is *away from* Jerusalem. For Luke the city and its temple are symbols of the people of Israel.

When gospel and Acts are, together, taken into account, one can appreciate Luke's purpose and achievement. Then one can see that his object was to present the definitive stage of God's saving plan from the birth of the Baptist to the proclamation of the gospel in the capital of the Gentile world – Rome. Acts is not, in the first place, a history of the Church; its first concern is the spread of the word of God. Luke's theme is the progress of the good news from Jerusalem to Rome. His is a message of salvation to the Gentiles. Simeon had seen in Jesus 'a light for revelation to the Gentiles' (Lk 2:32) and Paul's closing words to the Roman Jews are: 'Let it be known to you that this salvation of God has been sent to the Gentiles; they will listen' (Acts 28:28).

This concern does not eclipse the role of Israel. The beginning of the gospel attests that the church does not replace Israel. Himself come from Judaism, Jesus had striven, with the help of the Holy Spirit, to *renew* Israel. The salvation which he achieved and proclaimed meant that one be brought to God. He found that the marginalised – Galileans, women, 'sinners' – were more open to his challenge than the Judaeans and their leaders. But this offer was to all, for Israel needed saving as much as the Gentiles. In the gospel, after his account of the infancies of John and Jesus, Luke turned to the preaching of the rule of God, first by the precursor and then by the Messiah. At the close of his work he has Paul proclaiming the kingdom at the centre of the Roman world (Acts 28:30-31). The gospel tells of the mission of Jesus and of the saving event of his death and resurrection; it ends with his glorification at the ascension. Jesus had come as Messiah of his people and had found himself rejected by them. But his mission had not failed. He had brought salvation (Lk 24:47).

STORY

Luke is a gifted storyteller. Just think of the best-loved parables: the Prodigal Son, the Good Samaritan, Dives and Lazarus. While attributed by him to Jesus, and while they must, indeed, in substance, have come from Jesus, they surely have been shaped by Luke himself. Luke can and does work with a broader canvas. He forged an impressive narrative which started with a vision in the Jerusalem temple and ended at the heart of imperial Rome. 'Luke-Acts shows us an author of synthetic imagination, who was able to make the story of Jesus (already current in the church's tradition) and the story of Christianity's beginnings into one coherent and interconnected narrative which continued the ancient biblical story of God and his people.'[2]

Narrative Criticism

In the study of Luke-Acts, narrative criticism has particular relevance because Luke expressly describes his work as a *diegésis*, 'narrative,' (Lk 1:1). In narrative criticism 'meaning' is found in the encounter between the text and the reader. While narrative critics do not ignore the findings of historical-critical scholarship (for that matter, historical criticism and narrative criticism are complementary) they do ask different questions of the text. If the answer is, in each case, different, it is because the question is other. Narrative critics analyse Luke's gospel with reference to story and discourse. In other words, they look to the content of the narrative (story) and to how the story is told (discourse).

Luke-Acts was not written in a vacuum. The author was, naturally, influenced by established literary genres. In the first place, Luke-Acts resembles Hellenistic historical writing. This is, understandably, more evident in Acts. The many speeches there are typical of

the role of speeches in Hellenistic historiography. All of them are
Lucan compositions and are intended as commentary on related
events. Luke's work also resembles Jewish apologetic: in his presentation of the spread of the word, he sets himself to defend the
Christian movement.

THE GOSPEL

The point has been made that Luke-Acts is a single work, and this
will be kept in mind. The focus of this book, however, is the Jesus of
the *gospel*. We look, now, to the gospel alone. In the manner of the
Hellenistic writers of his day, Luke dedicated his book to a patron,
at the same time setting out the occasion, method and purpose of
his work. He does so in an elegant Greek which contrasts sharply
with the style of the immediately following chapters (his infancy
narratives). It is probable that the prologue (1:1-4) was meant to
introduce both parts of Luke's work and the brief reference in Acts
1:1 marks the link between both volumes and suggests the continuity of the whole. Luke had decided to write a gospel and had done
thorough preparatory research: he had carefully studied these
things 'from the beginning,' which meant going beyond the starting-point of the apostolic catechesis, the baptism of Jesus, to the
infancy of Jesus and of his precursor. His work will be 'orderly,'
with a theological rather than chronological order. Theophilus,
addressed as 'Most Excellent,' was a man of some social standing
who would help to promote the work. He himself could learn from
the gospel an appreciation of the solid foundation of the teaching he
had received.

Plot and Characters

A gospel, addressed to a Christian community, has the concerns
and needs of the community in mind. These are concerns and needs
perceived by the evangelist (not necessarily by the recipients or not,
at least, by all of them). His readers know the basic story as well as
the author. He makes his point by telling the story in his way. It is
story: with plot and characters. Each of the evangelists tells essentially the same story (manifestly true of the synoptists), but the
plots and emphases of the gospels differ considerably. The events
and actions of a story, its plot, regularly involve conflict; indeed
conflict (not necessarily violent conflict) is the heart of most stories.

Not alone do the gospels have plot but the plot is, in a sense, an evangelist's interpretation of the story. As writers of narrative literature, the evangelists achieved their purpose by means of plot and characterisation.

Characterisation refers to the manner in which a narrative brings characters to life in a story. In literary terms, 'characters' are not the same as people. In day-to-day life we know one another imperfectly. I may guess at your thoughts; I cannot really know what you are thinking. Characters can be transparent. The narrator may fully expose a character to the readers, can permit the reader to get inside the character. Alternatively, one can present a 'true' picture of any character. The gospels, in which Jesus is a literary character, make him known to us more profoundly than he, as a person, was in fact known to his contemporaries. Each gospel has several characters of varying importance for the flow of the story. Jesus is always the chief character; the evangelist speaks, primarily, through him. Jesus carries the central message of each gospel. And Jesus is chief spokesman of an evangelist's concern.

The plot of Luke revolves around conflict. The primary conflict is between Jesus and the religious authorities and reaches its culmination on the cross. In the infancy narrative (1:5-2:52) Luke, in characterising Jesus as Messiah, Son of God and Saviour, portrays him as an eschatological figure. The antagonistic religious authorities are described in sharp contrast to Jesus. The first encounter is, significantly, in the temple, the house of Jesus' Father and seat of the authorities' power. In 5:17-16:11, a cycle of five controversies (see Mk 2:1-3:6), the question of who holds real authority in Israel is raised. The tone of the 'conversation' is subdued – contrast the naked antagonism in Mk 3:6. This relatively mild tone continues up to chapter 19: the entry into Jerusalem and the cleansing of the temple (Lk 19:28-44, 45-46). Jesus, hailed as Israel's Messiah-King (v. 38), then takes over his temple (19:47; 20:1). At this point conflict with the religious authorities intensifies (19:47-21:38). They are out 'to kill' Jesus (19:47). By challenging them in the temple he struck at the root of their status as Israel's leaders. Their authority was in question (20:22, 27-33). Jesus effectively silenced them: 'They no longer dared to ask him another question' (20:40). At the close of the temptation story (4:13) Luke observed that the devil 'departed from him until an opportune time.' Now (22:1-6) Satan is back on the scene. The religious authorities brought about Jesus' death as instruments of Satan. The final confrontation is at 23:35 – 'The leaders scoffed at him, saying, "He saved others; let him save himself if he is the Messiah of God, his chosen one!"'

The last time the authorities confront the earthly Jesus, they abjectly repudiate him as being Israel's Messiah-King, regard him as bereft of all authority, see him as doomed to destruction, and are utterly convinced that, in their conflict with him, they have gained the victory and been vindicated as the rightful leaders of Israel.[3]

The resolution of the conflict is ironic: resurrection and ascension (ch 24) are God's vindication of Jesus. He is, after all, the one who holds universal authority.

Minister of the Word

Jesus had declared that he and his preaching were the fulfilment of what in the scriptures was associated with God's salvation. He stressed the radical character of the reaction to his kingdom preaching (Lk 16:16); he proclaimed 'salvation' (9:2). Christians had perceived that salvation was in him. The subject of their kingdom-preaching was Jesus himself: the crucified, risen and exalted Messiah, the Lord who is present to his followers through his Spirit. Luke has told the story of the Christ-event: Christ proclaimed in his fullness.

Luke, minister of the word (1:2), an evangelist, has remained faithful to the general plan of his pioneering predecessor, Mark. He has, however, made important changes in this order and so has given to his gospel quite another bias. He has prefaced the Marcan material with the long infancy narrative (chs 1-2) which, as an overture to the gospel, sounds many of the motifs to be orchestrated in gospel and Acts. Luke broke with Mark in what are known as the 'great omission' – the dropping of Mk 6:45-8:26 – and the interpolations: Lk 6:20-8:3 and 9:51-18:14. The latter, the 'great interpolation,' witnesses to his skill and his literary independence. Mark did have a rather hurried journey of Jesus to Jerusalem. Luke turned it into a leisured stroll during which Jesus had ample time to fit in varied teaching and a host of parables, most of them proper to Luke. In short, one must acknowledge that, despite general agreement with

Mark and Matthew, the third gospel is assertively distinctive. This is only to be expected. As we have observed, an evangelist, addressing a Christian community, is not telling the Jesus-story for the first time. The original reader/hearers know the lines of the story quite as well as the evangelist. What gave them pause was the question: why is the story presented in just this way? The challenge of the evangelist lay, precisely, in the distinctive slant.

Salvation History

Luke is a theologian of salvation history – the entrance of salvation into history. He alludes to a basic divine 'plan' for the salvation of humankind, one which was being realised in the activity of Jesus (7:30). The concept of such a plan is what underlies the 'necessity', e.g. 'Was it not necessary that the Messiah should suffer these things and then enter into his glory?' (24:26), which is often associated with what Jesus does or says and with what happens as fulfilment of scripture.[4] That the plan of God concerns the 'salvation' of humankind receives special emphasis in the Lucan writings.

For Luke, salvation history has three phases: a) period of Israel, from creation to the appearance of John the Baptist: the time of the law and the prophets (1:5 - 3:1); b) period of Jesus, from the baptism to the ascension of Jesus: the time of Jesus' ministry, death and exaltation (3:2 - 24:51); c) period of the church: the time of the spread of the word of God (Lk 24:52-Acts 28:31). If creation is the beginning and if the spread of the word will persist to the close of time, then Luke's understanding of salvation history is emphatically universalist. The new inbreaking of divine saving activity into human history includes the extension of salvation to persons outside of God's chosen people of old. The change involves a distinctive view of Israel. God has not replaced his chosen people with a new one. The church is not a new Israel but a reconstituted Israel with Gentiles taking their place beside Jews who had accepted the message of Jesus.

Salvation had come with Jesus. After the ascension, men and women would be saved through him and because of what he had accomplished. The events of the life of Jesus were decisive for the world, constituting the beginning of the last days. For Luke, Jesus was fulfilment of all the promises of God and that in spite of the

outward circumstances of his life which blinded the eyes of his contemporaries to the reality in their presence. This implied that all
that went before Jesus was preparatory. Yet, preparation, fulfilment
in Christ, and universal salvation through him in this age together
form one divine plan for the salvation of the world, a plan progres-
sively realised in history.

Christology

Lucan christology must be fitted into the pattern of Luke's salvation
history. Comparison of the conclusion of Matthew's gospel with
that of Luke alerts one to the remarkable theological pluralism of
the early church. In Matthew the risen Lord declares: 'Remember, I
am with you always, to the end of the age' (Mt 28:20). The Lucan
Jesus departs this world until the parousia (Lk 24:44-53; Acts 1:9-
11). At his Ascension Jesus had left his disciples, had taken his place
at the right hand of God. This fact leaves Luke free to concentrate
on the man of Nazareth who walked among us. We, who are so
tempted to short-cut the stark implication of the incarnation, would
be well advised to focus on Mark and Luke. If John it is who has
given us the notion of incarnation, it is Mark and Luke who stress
for us the humanness of the Son. Jesus is the human person in
whom God is definitively revealed for the salvation of humankind.

For Luke, Jesus is the eschatological prophet – a prophet who is also
the sage of Israelite tradition. As prophet it is not surprising that
Jesus (like Jeremiah) should face misunderstanding and opposition
nor that he should, in the end, meet violent death. Jesus did not die
a hero on the battlefield. He died, faithful prophet, a martyr's death.
Luke is intrigued by Jesus, fascinated by this man's concern for the
poor, the outcast.

The life of Jesus has its own thrust and forms a unity. Luke refuses
to single out any one event, not even the death of Jesus, and give it a
special saving significance. It is the whole life of this man which, by
the faith that it inspires and the 'following' that it challenges,
played a saving role: 'for the Son of Man came to seek out and save
the lost' (19:10). Consistently, after Easter, Luke focuses on the
struggles of Jesus' followers. His sequel to the story of Jesus is not
cast in the realm of the marvellous (though Luke does have a weakness for the 'marvellous' on a lesser scale) but in the reality, often

painful, of the Christian Way. There is nothing triumphalist about Luke.

For Luke the word of God was made flesh in Jesus but in another manner than for John. It is not the Johannine pre-existent Word but the word of God formerly addressed to the prophets that has taken flesh in Jesus (Acts 10:36-37). One may equally well say that in Jesus the flesh becomes word: the messenger becomes the message. In their turn the apostles carry on the incarnation of the word as they become the human suffering bearers of God's message. They carry the word differently from Jesus – in his name, not in their own.

The christological titles are a sign of the non-conformity of Jesus. In his *life* Jesus is conformed to the prophets of Israel. By the *titles* bestowed on him he stands radically apart from them. The incarnation of the word in his life has a specificity which the presence of God in the prophets and apostles does not carry. Thus the infancy gospel, far from being an appendage to Lucan christology, is where the lines of that christology come together. On this point, Luke is close to John. The theology of Luke is christological: it is linked to Easter and Ascension, because of the Passion – but also because of the Nativity.

Soteriology

Luke has told the Jesus-story not only with christological but with soteriological intent: what Jesus did, said and suffered had and has a significance for and a bearing on human history. Acts 4:12 makes this clear: 'There is salvation in no one else, for there is no other name under heaven given among mortals by which we must be saved.' It has been argued that Luke downplayed 'the cross'. In fact, reference to the death of Jesus in the Lucan work is impressive. Luke does not seek to suppress the tragedy and the mystery of the cross nor to underplay its saving role. He does not question the necessity for the disciple of Jesus to deny oneself, to take up the cross and to follow the Master (Lk 9:23; 14:27).

Then there is the manner in which Luke regards the effects of the Christ-event. 'Salvation' is evidently an important effect (see 19:10) While the verbal form 'to forgive sins' is frequent in the Synoptic: the abstract form 'forgiveness of sins' is a Lucan usage. Luke sur up Jesus' work as the release of men and women from their de (sins) in the sight of God. By all that he was and all that he did he has cancelled the debt incurred by their sinful conduct. In the sayings of Jesus 'peace' stands for the bounty he brings to humankind. And if he seems to deny that his coming brings peace (12:51), it is because he knows that men and women will have to make a decision about him, either for or against him. Those who accept him into their lives will know the peace which he alone can bring.

Dante named Luke *scriba mansuetudinis Christi* — the writer who had caught and portrayed the graciousness of Jesus. His Jesus had found in Isaiah 61:1-2 the programme of his mission. In his Nazareth synagogue Jesus opened the scroll of Isaiah and read out:

> The Spirit of the Lord is upon me
> because he has anointed me to bring good news to the poor.
> He has sent me to proclaim release to the captives
> and recovery of sight to the blind,
> to let the oppressed go free,
> to proclaim the year of the Lord's favour (Lk 4:18-19).

Then he declared: 'Today this scripture has been fulfilled in your hearing' (v. 21).[5] The Lucan Jesus displays a gracious concern for the 'little ones'. Instances leap to mind: the raising of a poor widow's son (7:11-17), welcome of the 'lost boy' (15:11-24), healing of a crippled woman (13:10-17). Most eloquent, perhaps, is Jesus' delicate response to the extravagant and brave gesture of the woman who had experienced his understanding and forgiving love (7:36-50). All the while, if there is great gentleness, there is nothing soft or easy-going about the Jesus of Luke. His demand is that one take up one's cross *daily*. And there is something almost shocking about his call for total renunciation, his invitation to give up *all* one has.

The Evangelist

Luke's spirituality is firmly inspired by his commitment to Jesus – that much is obvious. What matters is his commitment to the Jesus he *recognised*. And here is where Dante's observation is perceptively true. The Jesus of Luke is – though the title occurs only once (2:11) – Saviour. God's 'preferential option for the poor' might seem to be a new-fangled invention of Liberation Theology. In fact, it is a belated re-discovery of an option that was there from the first. No put-down of Liberation Theology; rather, a heartfelt 'thank you' to Liberation theologians for opening our eyes to what we should never have failed to see. The Lucan Jesus does indeed reflect the God who is readily recognisable in the Old Testament. He is, disconcertingly, God of sinners. Apart from the so-called judgment-scene of Matthew 25:31-46, there is no passage more subversive of Christian 'orthodoxy' than Lk 15:11-32. A 'sinner' is welcomed back into the home of his Father, welcomed without strings, welcomed at the word: 'I will get up and go.' The Father-God had yearned for an opening – he needed no more. Some time or other the church, so readily arbiter of 'reconciliation,' must really learn that the Father of Jesus is prodigal of forgiveness. Let us be honest about it: bishops and theologians have multiplied 'sins'. The God of Jesus knows that there is enough human misery and sin as it is. The Lucan Jesus, who really knows the Father, is wholly in the business of lifting the burden of sin – not of adding to it. That is why Jesus is Saviour.

What of the journey of Luke? He was one who had found, in Jesus, the inspiration and goal of his life. He viewed this Jesus in the light of his own temperament. It is, obviously, the 'softer' side of the character of Jesus that appealed to him. A distinctive feature of Luke-Acts is the prominence of women in the narrative: more women are listed in Luke than in the other three gospels together.[6] Luke's sensitivity to the 'poor' is not unrelated: in the world of his day women were among the poor, the marginalised. In the same spirit he was concerned for 'outcast' Samaritans (10:30-37; 17:11-19). After all, Jesus had come 'to preach good news to the poor' (4:18).

CHAPTER 2

Jesus

Therefore he had to become like his brothers and sisters in every respect ...
Because he himself was tested by what he suffered, he is able to help those
who are being tested (Heb 1:17-18)

'We believe in one Lord, Jesus Christ, the only Son of God ...' There
is a wealth of christology behind this credal statement, this proclamation of Christian faith. It is helpful – needful indeed – to map the
areas of faith and history. We find Jesus in both, as the 'real' Jesus
and as a scholarly construct. We learn from both perspectives. And
what we discern aids us in our appreciation of the Jesus of the
gospels. Here, in modest compass, we look to the 'historical' Jesus.

I. THE REAL JESUS

The object of Christian faith is the person of Jesus Christ who once
lived, briefly, on earth in the first century AD and now lives on in
the Father's presence. The gospels, at once historical and theological, proclaim Jesus of Nazareth as the Christ, the definitive revelation of God. The proclaimed Jesus is a construct of Christian theological and spiritual imagination aimed at eliciting a faith response.
The proclamation embraces strictly historical elements (e.g. Jesus'
death on the cross) and theological interpretation in terms of biblical categories (e.g. ascent to God's right hand).

> What [the gospels] give us is the Jesus-image, or the proclaimed
> Jesus who actually lived and died in first-century Palestine, who
> now reigns gloriously as Savior of the world, who indwells his
> followers of this and every age and who is the Christ in whom
> God is definitively and salvifically revealed ... The real Jesus is
> precisely the proclaimed Jesus. Part of the Jesus-image, and a
> constitutive and irreducible part, is the actual earthly career of
> Jesus of Nazareth that is the heart of the image.[7]

The real or actual Jesus is the glorified Saviour alive in our midst. He will always be shrouded in mystery. The total reality of any person is unknowable to human discernment – how much more the reality of the Risen One. The gospels present us with 'the earthly Jesus': a picture of Jesus during his life on earth. Their partial, and theologically coloured, pictures serve as the source for the theological construct 'the historical Jesus'. The historical Jesus is not the real Jesus but only a fragmentary hypothetical reconstruction of him by modern means of research. This is by no means to suggest that the result is of little importance. It is increasingly clear that the dangerous remembrance of this Jesus of flesh and blood is more needful than ever.

Theology, the study of faith, if it is to be credible and effective, must reflect the culture within which it takes shape. Modern christology, then, has to take cognisance of historical-critical concern and has to accomodate the quest for the historical Jesus. After all, if faith is adherence to a particular person, we will want to know all we can about this person. Besides, there has been a deep-rooted tendency, in the name of 'orthodoxy,' to stress so the divinity of Jesus that his humanity has almost been lost to sight. Christology has, in practice, ignored the life of Jesus or has seen little theological significance in it. Emphasis on the historical Jesus reminds us that the risen Christ is the same person who lived and suffered and died in first-century Palestine, a man as wholly human as any human person. Again, in Christian theology and practice, Jesus has been effectively domesticated. Historical research has brought to light a challenging and embarrassing non-conformist Jesus.

The historical Jesus is not coextensive with the Jesus of the gospel narratives. There is much in the gospel narratives that is not historical. The gospel picture is 'accurate' not in the sense that it is exact in detail but that it is truth-bearing. It is the acceptance of it by the early believing community that guarantees the substantial truth of the gospel account. The gospel Jesus is more than the historical Jesus: the gospel presents not only history but the transhistorical, not only fact but theological interpretation. On the other hand, the ecclesiastical proclamation of the Jesus-image is often less than, is unfaithful to, the historical Jesus in which the image is rooted. This is a further reason for investigation of and discernment of the historical Jesus.

II. THE HISTORICAL JESUS

Jesus of Nazareth was a first-century AD Jew who began, lived and ended his short life in Palestine, a minor province of the Roman Empire. Our information about him, by historical standards, is meagre. Apart from two brief statements, by the Jewish historian Flavius Josephus and the Roman historian Tacitus respectively, our sources for knowledge of the historical Jesus are the canonical gospels alone. A summary of the historical facts about Jesus of Nazareth, based on the meticulous research of a major New Testament scholar, will serve our purpose.[8]

Around 7-4 BC, that is, toward the end of the reign of Herod the Great, a Jewish boy, to be named Jesus (Yeshua), was born, either in Bethlehem of Judaea or Nazareth of Galilee. His mother was named Mary (Miryam), his putative father Joseph (Yosef). He grew up in Nazareth and was known as 'the Nazarene'. His native language was Aramaic; he would have had a practical command of Greek. It is highly likely that he was literate; as a boy he would have been taught in the village synagogue. Like Joseph (Mt 13:55), Jesus (Mk 6:3) was a *tektón* – most probably a carpenter. In a small village, Joseph's would have been the only carpenter shop; the family would have had a frugally comfortable lifestyle.

The gospels speak of the 'brothers (and sisters)' of Jesus. The most striking passage is Mk 6:3 – 'Is not this the carpenter, the son of Mary and brother of James and Judas and Simon, and are not his sisters here with us?' Throughout the New Testament the word *adelphos* ('brother'), when not used metaphorically, means a blood brother – whether full or half brother. It is most natural, then, to regard these brothers and sisters of Jesus as his siblings. It is, nonetheless, not unreasonable, on theological grounds, to take the term in a broader sense. At the same time, it should be noted that the tradition of the virginal conception of Jesus (which, strictly speaking, would not necessarily exclude his having brothers and sisters) is found only in the Infancy Narratives (Mt 1-2; Lk 1-2) – and these are profoundly christological texts. The point is: a definite answer to these questions is beyond the scope of historical-critical research. But the questions are there.

Not controversial is the fact that Jesus of Nazareth was a layman, who lived in the quiet obscurity of a Galilean village. It is not surprising that the gospels (outside the Passion Narratives) show no evidence of any dialogue with the Jerusalem priests. They would have had no interest in a Galilean layman – until they began to perceive him as a threat. The letter to the Hebrews does, of course, elaborate a theology of the priesthood of Christ. It is precisely that: a theological construct – the heavenly priesthood of the Risen One. The author is perfectly aware that the earthly Jesus was not a priest:

> Now if he were on earth, he would not be a priest at all, since there are priests who offer gifts according to the law (8:4).

> It is evident that our Lord was descended from Judah, and in connection with that tribe Moses said nothing about priests (7:14).

In our western world we have a fascination with dates and times – birthdays, and so on. When one really thinks about it, such precision is not of much importance. I was born, I will die – this is the reality that is mightily important to me. Marks on a calendar are of little significance. It matters little that we are unable to date precisely the birth, ministry and death of Jesus. We may, at best, propose a fair approximation:

Birth	7-6 B.C.
Beginning of Ministry	AD 28. If Jesus began his ministry early in 28, it would have lasted a little over two years.
Death	AD 30. 14 Nisan – eve of Passover. Jesus would have been about thirty-six at his death.

We turn to some aspects of Jesus' ministry and death.

III. DISCIPLE OF THE BAPTIST

In all four gospels, before the ministry of Jesus opens, John the Baptist is introduced. According to the synoptic gospels (not, however, in the fourth gospel) Jesus was baptised by John. Who is this John? In his *Jewish Antiquities* the Jewish historian Flavius Josephus writes of the execution of John by Herod Antipas. He has it in the context of the defeat of Herod by the Nabatean King Aretus IV in 36 AD. In his judgment the defeat was retribution for Herod's slaying of John. He describes John, surnamed the Baptist, as one who baptised Jews who 'were cultivating virtue and practising justice toward one another and piety toward God'. Because John had won a notable following, Herod feared that his popularity might spark a revolt. He decided on a pre-emptive strike and had John arrested and sent in chains to Machaerus, a fortress south of the Dead Sea. There John was put to death. This account of the death of the Baptist is preferable to the evidently legendary story of Mk 6:17-29.

John the Baptist

It is clear from Josephus' text (and he has more to say of the Baptist than of Jesus) that John had been a prominent figure. This is borne out by the gospels. Paradoxically, they witness to the importance of the Baptist by consistently cutting him down to size. In Mk (1:2-11) the Baptiser is he who would prepare the way for 'one who is more powerful than I'. He was unaware that Jesus was the mightier one. In Matthew (3:13-15) John recognised Jesus' status and acknowledged his own inferiority. In Luke (1:41-44; 3:19-21) Jesus, cousin of John, met with John; it is not explicitly stated that he was baptised by John; the implication is there. In the fourth gospel John is not given the title Baptist – there is an oblique reference to his practice of baptising (1:25-26). There is no place for the baptism of Jesus by John. Here the *raison d'être* of John is to witness to Jesus (Jn 1:7-8, 19, 23, 29, 34; 3:29-30).

It is evident that early Christians were increasingly uneasy at this baptism of their Jesus by the Baptist – embarrassment is evident in Mt 3:13-14. The reaction underlines the firm historicity of the occurrence: they were stuck with the fact. The matter is complicated by the characterisation of John's baptism as 'a baptism of repentance for the forgiveness of sins' (Mk 1:4). This made Jesus' submission to John's baptism even more problematic. In John's estimation, however, his baptism was not only a sign of the candidates' repentance but pledge of new life, of a radical change. It was too, symbolically, an anticipation of an ultimate total cleansing of sin. In this perspective, a Jesus who was not conscious of sin could accept baptism from John.

John, in short, emerges as an eschatological prophet: he proclaimed the imminence of the end, marked by fiery judgment. This is a distinctively apocalyptic view. In apocalyptic perspective there is, in our world, a war to the death between good and evil. Good will surely triumph. Evil, and all evildoers, will perish in final judgmental conflagration. Now is the time of decision. The tone of the Baptist's clarion call (in Matthew and Luke) is characteristic of apocalyptic: 'You brood of vipers! Who warned you to flee from the wrath to come? ... Even now the axe is lying at the root of the trees ... every tree that does not bear good fruit is cut down and thrown into the fire ... His winnowing fork is in his hand ... the chaff he will burn with unquenchable fire' (Mt 3:10-12; see Lk 3:7-9). In Matthew (3:11-12) the agent of this fiery judgment is a coming one 'who is more powerful' than the Baptist. In Mk 1:7-8 the 'more powerful one' will (on the last day) baptise with the Holy Spirit, that is, wholly cleanse the repentant sinner. John does not specify who this 'stronger one' is.

The evidence, from Josephus and the gospels (see Mt 11:2-29; Lk 7:18-35), substantiates the impression that John the Baptist, a Jewish prophet, had gained a reputation and a following. For very different reasons he attracted the attention of Herod Antipas and of Jesus of Nazareth. His ministry preceded that of Jesus – who indeed, for a time, became involved in it. And this movement did not end with his death but continued apart from the Christian movement (see Acts 18:24- 19:7). John was worthy of the accolade of Jesus: 'Truly I tell you, among those born of women no one has arisen greater than John the Baptist' (Mt 11:11; see Lk 7:28).

Disciple of the Baptist

The starting-point for any account of the ministry of Jesus of Nazareth is his encounter with John the Baptist: the call which Jesus heard when he was baptised by John and to which he responded. By submitting to baptism Jesus became, in effect, a disciple of the Baptist.[9] John had begun his mission in the wilderness (Lk 3:2) of Peraea, beyond the Jordan, appearing where Elijah had disappeared (2 Kgs 2) and forcing the question of his identity (Mk 1:6). A wilderness audience would consist of travellers on an established route; a receptive audience would be Galilean pilgrims – avoiding hostile Samaria in a roundabout way to Jerusalem (see Lk 9:51-53). Jesus, very likely, had heard of the eschatological prophet. Now, as a Galilean pilgrim, he encountered this strange and striking man, who wore a camel-hair cloak bound with a leather belt: an Elijah-figure. Jesus received baptism and stayed with John – as Elisha had become a disciple of Elijah. Later, some of John's disciples, whether or not at his instigation, transferred to Jesus (Jn 1:35-42).

Some statements in the fourth gospel imply much more than might appear at first sight. Take John 3:22-23 – 'After this Jesus and his disciples went into the Judaean countryside, and he spent some time there with them and baptised. John was also baptising at Aenon near Salim [in Samaria].' We could take this to mean that John had sent Jesus into Judaea while he had gone to the more challenging Samaria. That the ministry of Jesus involved baptism is explicit in 3:22 and 4:1 – 'Now when Jesus had heard, "Jesus is making and baptising more disciples than John..."' The observation reflects a later dispute as to the relative merits of John's and Jesus' baptisms. It is obvious that 4:2 – 'although it was not Jesus himself but his disciples who baptised' – is a maladroit redactional 'correction'. Evidently, the concern was to distance Jesus from the Baptist.

Later, John moved into Galilee, territory of Herod Antipas, and was promptly arrested. The observation in Jn 4:3 is significant: '[Jesus] left Judaea and started back to Galilee.' The Baptist had been silenced. Jesus moved in to take his place: *noblesse oblige*. What emerges from all this is that, at first, Jesus was disciple of, and in the line of, the Baptist. At some time there was a radical change. The point seems to have been reached with Jesus' welcome for sinners. Although he admired John, Jesus was to follow his own way. John was a prophet of doom who preached 'a baptism of repentance for the forgiveness of sins' (Mk 1:4) – and we need to keep in mind that Jesus, too, baptised. On the other hand, Jesus proclaimed: 'The kingdom of God has come near' (1:15). It is a matter of emphasis. Where John prophesied the judgment of God, Jesus prophesied the salvation of God. Hearing, in prison, of the activity of Jesus, a perplexed John sent two of his disciples to investigate. Jesus' reply was: 'Go and tell John what you have seen and heard: the blind receive their sight, the lame walk, the lepers are cleansed, the deaf hear, the dead are raised, the poor good news brought to them' (Lk 7:22). One can read between the lines. John was being told that there was another prophetic message, another prophetic style. One might put it that John was in the line of Amos – that prophet of unrelieved gloom. Jesus was in the line of Hosea, prophet of God's gracious love. We must not, however, overlook the fact that Jesus, like Hosea, also spoke words of warning.

The baptism of Jesus by John is certainly historical; note the embarrassment of Mt 3:13-15. We look to the implication of it. In the first place, it indicated a fundamental change in Jesus' life: he became a disciple of the Baptist. He had come to know the eschatological message of John and showed, by his adherence, his basic acceptance of it. He submitted to John's baptism as a seal on his decision to change his manner of life. Hitherto, he had been a village carpenter; henceforth he would be proclaimer of the word. He would preach *metanoia*, a radical change of heart, in a wholehearted striving to renew Israel. The baptism launched him on a road that would eventually lead to the cross – though, surely, this prospect did not then appear on his horizon.

IV. THE MINISTRY

At some point Jesus, one-time disciple of John the Baptist, did strike out on his own. According to the general run of the gospel narratives, he was engaged during the early part of his ministry in three main types of activity:

— He was engaged upon a broad appeal to the public. His aim was to make people aware of the presence of God as an urgent reality and to invite their appropriate response. In this he echoed in some measure the clarion call of the Baptist.

— He set himself to minister to human need by healing the sick, exorcising evil and awakening hope in those who had lost hope. And he sought to lead men and women into new life under the inspiration of a personal attachment to himself. By going about doing good he gave concrete shape to his message of the rule of God – of ultimate salvation.

— While his ministry cast him, in part, as teacher, his outlook and approach differentiated him from rabbinic Judaism. He challenged people to rethink their ideas and hopes, only to be branded a heretic. He censured his contemporaries, and, in particular, the religious authorities, for shrugging off God's warnings. In his mission, controversy was forced upon him.

Jesus did not come preaching a 'new religion'; he came to renew

Israel. His call was for *metanoia*, a radical change of heart. He had
come to summon Israel to become what God had wanted his people
to be. He had caught up the urgent call of the Baptist and had made
it his own. He was quite clear as to his goal: 'I was sent only to the
lost sheep of the house of Israel' (Mt 15:24; see 10:5-6). Inherent in
Jesus' vision, however, was a dimension that, eventually, would no
longer fit in the old wineskins.

Jesus began his mission with optimism. He did not start off with a
vision of violent death at the end of the road. But, as his mission
progressed, he had to come to terms with the reaction and opposition that forced him to reckon with, first, the possibility and, then,
the probability, of a violent end. It is likely that the temptation
stories, put before the start of the ministry by Luke and Matthew,
really concern decisions made at a later date. Certainly, Gethsemane and the anguished cry on the cross (Mk 14:32-42; 15:34) –
hardly to be thought of as Christian refinements – witness to the
agony of decision and the depressing prospect of failure.

It is not surprising that, in the atmosphere of the day, Jesus might
have been, in some measure, viewed as a messianic figure.
Messianic pretensions were urged by the religious authorities in
their action against Jesus. They badly needed to present him (to
Pilate) as constituting a political threat; the political overtones of
messianism would serve. It is, moreover, likely that Jesus' opponents may have understood him or his followers to claim that he was
the Messiah. Jesus himself did not claim to be Messiah – nor did he
ever deny the role. It is very likely that some of his followers
thought him to be the Messiah. It is evident that, after the resurrection, Jesus was, by his followers, regularly called the Messiah –
Jesus Christ (Messiah).

V. DEATH AND BURIAL

The ministry of Jesus ended in final conflict with religious and
political authority. Jesus was condemned to death by Pilate. He was
promptly scourged: a severe flogging was a normal prelude to crucifixion. Death by crucifixion was, and was intended to be, degrading. Even the choice of the place of Jesus' execution was calculated
insult. Archaeology has shown that Golgotha, a disused quarry,
was, at that time, a refuse-dump. There was nothing of majesty

about the death of Jesus, no trace of glory. It was customary for the condemned man to carry his cross beam. A certain Simon of Cyrene was recruited to assist Jesus. It was Jewish custom, prompted by Proverbs 31:6-7, to provide condemned victims with drugged wine; Jesus did not take the wine. By custom, the clothes of the condemned, if of any value, fell to the executioners. A superscription on the cross was in accordance with Roman practice. Mark has Jesus crucified at the third hour (9 a.m.). He died at the ninth hour (3 p.m.) (Mk 15:25,34). Jesus had spent six hours in agony. Yet, his death came surprisingly early; crucified victims normally lingered much longer.

The disciples of Jesus (except for some women – and they stood well apart from the scene) had fled at his arrest; it was left to another to bury him. Joseph of Arimathea, a Sanhedrin member, was concerned to fulfil the law – here that the body of one hanged (displayed) should not be left overnight on the tree (Deut 21:23). (In Mt 27:57 and Jn 19:38 Joseph is said to have been a disciple of Jesus – a manifest later development.) Joseph was duly granted the corpse of Jesus (Mk 15:42-46). It would be a hurried, dishonourable burial of one sentenced to death on a charge of blasphemy. The body was not anointed. It was simply wrapped in a shroud and placed in a niche of the disused quarry that was Golgotha. A far cry, indeed, from the royal burial of the fourth gospel (Jn 19:38-42). What matters is that the burial, for all its finality, was not the end. 'He is going ahead of you to Galilee...' (Mk 16:7).

CHAPTER 3

Birth of the Messiah

The infancy narratives of Matthew and Luke have had a notable influence on Christian tradition and have found remarkable scope in Christian art. The long appreciation of them has not been mis-placed. We had sensed that there was something special here – that these texts said quite a lot more than they appeared to say. In our day we have, happily, come to realise that both infancy narratives – which are wholly independent of each other – are, first and fore-most, christological statements. It is along this line, and only here, that we can grasp their true meaning.

Our concern is Luke's infancy narrative (chapters 1-2).[10] Because this text is a literary unit we will look to the whole of it, while the focus will be on the Jesus' sections. Luke, writing consciously in the style of the Septuagint (the Greek Old Testament), composed his narrative in two stages. The first stage established a parallelism between the Baptist and Jesus, with two annunciations of concep-tion (Lk 1:5-56) and two narratives of birth-circumcision-naming-promise (1:57-2:40). At a later stage Luke inserted the canticles, Benedictus, Magnificat and Gloria (1:46-55; 1:68-79; 2:29-32) and added the episode of the finding in the temple (2:41-52) – valuable material which, however, unbalanced the neat pattern of diptychs, the arrangement in parallel panels.

The original plan brings home Luke's intention. John the Baptist and Jesus are compared and contrasted, but the greatness of Jesus is emphasised even by the more developed account of his origins. Within the parallel narratives the same point is made. Mary is clearly shown to be superior to Zechariah and, more explicitly, the son of Mary is set on a pedestal and towers above the son of Zechariah. The parent cell of these two chapters is the infancy of Jesus and, more precisely, the Annunciation. The infancy of the Baptist is a prelude, composed by Luke, in order that the Messiah may be introduced by his precursor as in the gospel tradition of the ministry.

The infancy narrative of Luke, no less than that of Matthew, is firmly christological. In 1:31 Mary is told that she is to be mother of a son named Jesus who, in vv. 32-33, is designated the Davidic Messiah, in terms taken from 2 Samuel 7:9-16. Luke uses the technique of Mary's question and Gabriel's answer (1:34-35) to point to the true identity of Jesus: he is son of David and Son of God. It is Luke's dramatic version of an early christological formula such as Rom 1:3-4 – the 'son, who was descended from David according to the flesh and was declared to be Son of God with power ... by resurrection from the dead.'

Prophecy of John's Birth (1:5-25)

The introduction of the episode (1:5-7) gives four items of information. The first three – time setting in the reign of Herod the Great, the names Zechariah and Elizabeth, their priestly descent – are items of tradition. The other, that they were aged and Elizabeth barren, echoes the stories of Abraham and Sarah, Elkanah and Hannah (Gen 15:17-19; 1 Sam 1). Thus, the birth of John the Baptist is in continuity with the birth of famous figures in the salvific history of Israel.

The pattern of annunciation (Lk 1:11-20) reflects the announcing of the births of Ishmael (Gen 16), Isaac (Gen 17) and Samson (Jdgs 13) and carries echoes of Dan 8:16-27; 9:21-23. The Lucan angel is named Gabriel (as in Daniel). The verses 15-17, which prophetically characterise the adult Baptist as an ascetic prophet summoning Israel to repentance, are culled from the ministry portrayal of him – 3:1-3; 7:24-35. The sign, required by the literary pattern, is dumbness, suggested by Dan 10:15. Since Elizabeth's pregnancy is going to be a sign for Mary (1:36) her seclusion (1:24-25) underlines the sign-value since no one could have known of her pregnancy. For Zechariah and Elizabeth, Luke looked to the Old Testament models of Abraham and Sarah; for the infant Baptist he drew on the description of John in his gospel story of the ministry. He has portrayed the Baptist in conscious parallel to Jesus – taking consistent care to keep the former on a lower level.

Prophecy of Jesus' Birth (1:26-38)

The structure again follows faithfully the Old Testament pattern of annunciation of birth. Hence, material not explained by the literary pattern is significant: the peculiar manner of conception (virginal), identity of the child (vv. 32-33, 35), the portrait of Mary in vv. 34 and 38. In 1:32-33 Jesus is described as the Davidic Messiah in terms taken from 2 Sam 7:9-16. The only thing specifically Christian here is that Jesus has been identified as that promised Messiah. Mary's question and Gabriel's answer speak Luke's christological message. The Messiah is God's Son and his conception is not through marital intercourse (Mary) but through the Holy Spirit (Gabriel). See Rom 1:3-4.

The portrait of Mary in 1:38 is shaped from Luke's account of her in the ministry; as one who hears and does the will of God she is truly 'servant of the Lord'. Luke sees Mary as summing up in her person the deepest and purest traditions of Old Testament piety. She was one of those whose trust was not in an external, political redemption. Over the centuries the expectation of deliverance had been purified and spiritualised and there was a class who yearned for a deeper and more personal salvation – the *anawim*. Mary was of this tradition. The annunciation of Jesus' birth is, also, in some sort, a commissioning of Mary as the first Christian disciple. Against the patriarchal background of Luke's biblical tradition, his focus on Mary is striking. It carries a typical Lucan message.

> In contrast to Zechariah, we notice, Mary holds no official posi-
> tion among the people, she is not described as 'righteous' in
> terms of observing Torah, and her experience did not take place
> in a cultic setting. She is among the most powerless people in
> her society: she is young in a society that values age; female in a
> world ruled by men; poor in a stratified economy. Furthermore,
> she has neither husband nor child to validate her existence. That
> she should have found 'favour with God' and be 'highly gifted'
> shows Luke's understanding of God's activity as surprising and
> often paradoxical, almost always reversing human expecta-
> tions.[11]

Virginal conception is patently proposed by Matthew (1:18-25). Is it as clear in Luke? Yes, if the contrast of Baptist and Jesus is given due weight. John is 'great in the sight of the Lord' (Lk 1:15a), Jesus is 'great', without qualification (1:32a). John is 'filled with the Holy Spirit even before his birth' (1:15), the very conception of Jesus involves the Holy Spirit that 'comes upon' his mother (1:35). John will 'make ready a people prepared for the Lord' (1:17), Jesus will rule over the house of Jacob-Israel and possess an eternal kingdom (1:33). John's conception is miraculous (1:7,18). If the conception of Jesus were normal then John has moved up a step. But, if the conception of Jesus is not only miraculous but virginal the careful pattern is preserved. It is noteworthy that, just as Luke declares the age and barrenness theme in 1:7 and has Zechariah repeat it in 1:18, he describes Mary as a virgin in 1:27 and has her own attestation of it in 1:34. He thus draws our attention to his assertion of virginal conception.

All very well, but how is 'virginal conception' to be understood? It is to be noted that in each infancy narrative the second chapter (Mt 2; Lk 2), read by itself, would not in the least suggest virginal conception. There is no echo of the claim elsewhere in the New Testasment, but it later became widely accepted in Christian belief. One must endorse the need, in our day, of candidly seeking to grasp what the credal formula *natus ex Maria virgine* really intends to say. Is it a *theologoumenon* (a theological insight narrated as a factual event) – or does it necessarily demand biological virginity? What is not in doubt is that both Matthew and Luke are primarily interested in virginal conception as the expression of a christological insight that Jesus was God's son in a unique sense.

Mary Visits Elizabeth (1:39-56)

In the structure of the Lucan infancy narrative this passage, 'The Visitation,' is a complementary episode, a pendant to the diptych of annunciations (1:5-38). Elizabeth was granted the perception not only that Mary is with child but that her child is the Messiah. Her canticle in praise of Mary (1:42-45) echoes Old Testament motifs and anticipates motifs that will be found in the gospel (11:27-28). This narrative serves as a hinge between the two birth stories of John and of Jesus. And this meeting of women illustrates their respective situations.

At Mary's greeting Elizabeth felt the infant stir within her – John, while still in the womb, is precursor (1:17) of the Lord. Enlightened by the prophetic Spirit, she concluded that Mary is to be mother of 'the Lord.' That is why Mary is 'blessed among women' – the most blessed of women. Elizabeth went on to praise Mary's unhesitating acquiescence in God's plan for her – her great faith: 'And blessed is she who believed...' The song of Mary (1:46-55) – echoing the song of Hannah in 1 Sam 2:1-10 – moves from the reversal of Mary's condition from lowliness to exaltation (vv. 47-49), on to a general statement of God's mercy (v. 50). Then a recital of his past and present reversals (vv. 51-53) and a final statement on his mercy to Israel in fulfilment of his promise to Abraham (vv. 54-55). In some sort, throughout, Mary is representative of Israel. Mary's Magnificat anticipates the preaching and practice of the Lucan Jesus in the body of the gospel. It refers to the reversal of values made explicit in the Beatitudes and Woes (6:20-26) and given expression in his own conduct.

The Birth of John (1:57-80)

The birth of John marked the fulfilment of the angel's message to Zechariah. Circumcision was prescribed for the eighth day after birth. Elizabeth, to the consternation of relatives who had objected to her choice of name, was supported by her husband: the child's name was John. At that Zechariah found himself able to speak again. The infancy story of the Baptist closes (1:80) with a 'refrain of growth' indicating his physical and spiritual development. In typical Lucan style, reference to John's sojourn in the desert prepares the way for his next appearance (3:2). The canticle of Zechariah (1:68-79) begins with the fulfilment of God's promised visitation of his people and then focuses on John's role as 'prophet of the Most High'. The canticles play a role analogous to that of speeches in Hellenistic historical writings (or the speeches in Acts): they interpret the narrative events. As canticles they are early Jewish Christian compositions taken over and adapted by Luke.

The Birth of Jesus (2:1-21)

The setting (2:1-7) is necessitated in part by Luke's assumption that Joseph and Mary lived in Nazareth before Jesus was born; Matthew has their home in Bethlehem. Luke must get Mary to Bethlehem for the birth of Jesus. His stratagem is the census of Quirinius and he is certainly confused in his account of the census – an unhistorical event as he relates it.[12] But, then, it may be that we have tended to take Luke too literally. His prime interest would seem to lie in the fact that the mighty Augustus – 'in those days a decree went out from the Emperor Augustus that all the world should be registered' (2:1) – was, unwittingly, an instrument of the Lord (a thoroughly biblical theme). Through it came to pass that Jesus the Messiah was born in the town of David. When we look at it dispassionately we must admit that what we had taken to be the Lucan picture of many distant descendants of David crowding into insignificant Beth-lehem is not very likely – still less likely as a policy of the practical Romans. What Luke wants to show is that Jesus was born in the hometown of David as one who belonged there – not in lodgings like an alien. Manger and swaddling clothes (2:12) symbolise God's care and protection. They may have a further resonance. 'Can the threefold, deliberate phrasing in the Greek of, "wrapped him in cloth strips, placed him in a manger, because there was no place," perhaps anticipate the same threefold rhythm of "wrapped him in a linen cloth, placed him in a rock-hewn tomb, where no one had yet been laid" (23:53) so that birth and burial mirror each other?'[13]

From the first, Mary was a caring mother, solicitously wrapping her baby and laying him in a manger-cradle. Luke is not suggesting anything miraculous about the birth; he simply shows that the 'ser-vant of the Lord' was, in her loving care, reflecting God's care. In the annunciation to the shepherds (2:8-14) heaven and earth touch. It is fitting that shepherds, reminiscent of the shepherd David, should be first to hear the news that a Saviour has been born in Bethlehem. The angels interpreted the event and gave it its true meaning: this child is Saviour, Messiah and Lord. The form of the proclamation (vv. 10-11) and the canticle, the Gloria (v. 14), would seem, again, to glance at Augustus who, architect of the *pax Augusta,* was hailed as Saviour. Jesus, not he, Luke asserts, is Saviour and bringer of peace.

The splendour of angelic manifestation and heavenly glory at his birth was not reflected in the person of Jesus: he is the infant, lying helpless in a manger, a baby who will be circumcised on the eighth day (2:21). This contrast – between helplessness and splendour – can be seen to anticipate the death of Jesus, helpless on the cross, and his subsequent resurrection and ascension to the Father. One can look to the words of the risen Lord on the road to Emmaus: 'Was it not necessary that the Messiah should suffer these things and then enter into his glory?' (24:26). Luke's infancy narrative teaches us, in its way, what Paul and Mark urge, that we must let God be God. A manger is as foolish as the cross. But in the one, as in the other, we encounter the wisdom of God. At the beginning, as at the end, we meet helplessness: a new-born babe imprisoned in tight swaddling-bands, and that child, now a man, nailed helplessly to a cross. In the swaddled baby and in the crucified man God is challenging us to acknowledge him as the God who thrives in weakness, and to recognise ourselves in the human person who was wholly open to that weakness which is the only strength.

In the reaction (2:15-20) to birth and heavenly proclamation, the shepherds are forerunners of future believers who will glorify God for what they had heard and will praise God for what they had seen. In this third part of the passage all the protagonists, Mary, Joseph, baby and the shepherds, come together. Yet, only one figure constitutes a bridge from the infancy narrative to the ministry of Jesus, and that is Mary, his mother. She is that by being a believer and disciple (Lk 8:19-21; 11:27-28; Acts 1:12-14). This is what Luke intends by his declaration: Mary 'treasured all these words and pondered them in her heart' (2:19). One should look to the parallel assertion in 2:51 – 'His mother treasured all these things in her heart.' She, like the Twelve, will come to full understanding when Jesus will have risen from the dead. Until then, in the obscurity of faith, she pondered these puzzling events. It is a misunderstanding of Luke's purpose, and of his literary achievement, to claim, as some have argued, that these statements point to Mary as source of the evangelist's narrative. Luke has access to some traditions, but the infancy narrative, as we have it, is his creation.

The Presentation (2:22-40)

In Matthew's infancy narrative the magi story displays the magi reacting with acceptance and homage to the proclamation of the birth of the Messiah (Mt 2:1-12). Luke's shepherds play a similar role. But the magi story has two elements missing in the Lucan story up to now: the positive response of Gentiles (the magi) and the rejection of the new-born Messiah by Herod and the chief priests and scribes (Mt 2:3-4). These are supplied in Simeon's double oracle

(Lk 2:29-32, 34-35). In the setting of this episode (2:22-24) Luke has combined two separate Israelite customs: (1) consecration or presentation of the child (Ex 13:1, 11-16); (2) purification of the mother after the birth of a child (Lev 12:1-8). Luke's text gives evidence of his general knowledge of these rituals and his inaccurate grasp of details. Simeon's Nunc Dimittis introduces the theme of salvation for the Gentiles (see Is 42:6; 52:10). In the second oracle (2:34-45) Simeon anticipates the rejection of Jesus by the Jewish authorities and the rejection of the Christian mission to Israel as described in Acts. Here is where the mother is drawn into the destiny of her son. He will be a 'sign of contradiction,' a challenge; the thoughts of those hostile to Jesus will come to light. Mary stands among the smaller group of those who will 'rise' rather than of those who will 'fall'. She, a daughter of Israel, will be tested like the rest. She cannot be different from her son, the one who 'in every resepct has been tested as we are' (Heb 4:15). Mary, too, will be tested and, like him, prove faithful.

Simeon can die in peace like Abraham (Gen 15:15) but more privileged than Abraham. His cup is overflowing because he has gazed upon the 'salvation' of God, the Messiah whom God had sent to save his people. And not his own people only: the Gentiles, too, are destined for salvation (Lk 2:29-32; see Is 52:10; 42:6; 49:6). This messianic salvation is not only a beacon which shines before the nations, it is a brightness which dissipates their darkness and enlightens them. In his manner, Luke has made the point that the son of David is also son of Abraham (see Mt 1:1). And, in his genealogy (3:23-38) Luke, working backwards, has Jesus as 'son of Adam, son of God' (3:38).

Luke has a litany of christological titles in these chapters. The child is son of David; he is Messiah. He is Son of God: leader of God's covenant people, with a unique relationship to the Father. As such, he is Lord. He is Saviour. Luke uses this latter title only once in his gospel, in the word of the angel to the shepherds: 'To you is born this day a Saviour' (2:11). The title is not repeated, but it is noteworthy that the evangelist has drawn attention to the name given to the child at his circumcision – Jesus ('Yahweh saves'). At any rate, the Christ of Luke is throughout, and before all else, a Saviour who is full of compassion and tenderness and great forgiveness.

'This child is destined for the falling and the rising of many in Israel, and to be a sign that will be opposed' (2:34). Though the infant has come as the Saviour of his people he will be rejected by many of them. The point is well made in the fourth gospel: 'He came to what was his own, and his own people did not accept him' (1:11). He will stand as a sign of contradiction, a stone that can be stumbling-block (Is 8:14-15) or cornerstone (Is 28:16) according as people turn their backs on him or accept him (Lk 2:34-35). As usual, Luke is anticipating the reaction that Jesus encountered in his ministry: 'Do you think that I have come to bring peace to the earth? No, I tell you, but rather division!' (12:51). There is the reaction of his own Nazareth neighbours (4:16-30): 'They drove him out of the town, and led him to the brow of the hill on which their town was built, so that they might hurl him off the cliff' (4:29). Luke has in mind, also, rejection of the Christian mission to Israel, a recurring feature in Acts. It is enough to note the Lucan Paul's closing words to Israel (Acts 28:25-28) – 'Let it be known to you that this salvation of God has been sent to the Gentiles: they will listen' (v. 28).

The child is an occasion of 'falling and rising'; there are two groups because Jesus is an abiding challenge. Again, the Johannine view is relevant. There can be no neutrality, because Jesus is the light that people cannot ignore (see Jn 9:39; 12:44, 50), the light that reveals their inmost thoughts and forces them to take part for him or against him. It is significant that 'falling' comes first – recognition of the fact, lamented by Paul (Rom 9-11), that only a handful in Israel hearkened to the good news. The sad truth is, Jesus will ever be a sign of contradiction.

The Boy Jesus in the Temple (2:41-52)

This passage, concerning a twelve-year old Jesus, is scarcely an infancy story and the repeated conclusion in v. 52 (see v. 40) marks it as an addition. It helps Luke to temper somewhat the otherwise total silence from infancy to the start of Jesus' ministry (3:23). Originally, the story seemed to situate the 'christological moment,' the understanding of who Jesus really is, in Jesus' youth: here we have Jesus say of himself what the heavenly voice will say at baptism (3:22). Obviously, for Luke, the punchline is v. 49: 'Did you not know that I must be in my Father's house?' Jesus, in his first spoken words in Luke's gospel, himself announces who he is: he is the one totally committed to God, his Father. By stressing Mary's lack of understanding (v. 50) Luke makes the historically accurate assertion that the christology of Jesus as God's Son was not perceived until after the resurrection.

> Luke shows the reader that even the most faithful of the people 'did not understand' in the time of the prophet's first visitation. The reader is also reminded that just as Jesus must 'progress' in wisdom, so must those who follow his story, who, like Mary, 'keep these words in their heart.'[14]

CONCLUSION

The Letter to the Hebrews presents Jesus as a Son who 'had to become like his brothers and sisters in every respect' (2:17), a Son who 'in every respect has been tested as we are, yet without sin' (4:15). He is the human being who stands in a relationship of obedient faithfulness towards God (3:16) and who stands in solidarity with human suffering. Thereby he is mediator: a true priest who can bring humankind to God. If he bears 'the exact imprint of God's very being' (1:3) it is because we see in him what makes God God; he shows us that God is God of humankind. He had come to do the saving will of the Father and had learned God's purpose 'through what he suffered' (5:8). In Gethsemane he had prayed 'with loud cries and tears to the one who was able to save him from death' (5:7); he came to understand that the way of faithfulness led to the cross. Jesus, in his life and fate, lived the truth of Simeon's word – he was indeed a sign of contradiction.

We are not surprised to learn that what Jesus was throughout his adult life he had been from the start. If his conception was unique in that it was virginal, there was nothing remarkable about his birth. He came into the world with a cry, as every baby does. He had to be fed and clothed and cared for. He was 'born of a woman' (Gal 4:4) – he had entered fully into the human situation in all its vulnerability. Furthermore, 'born under the law,' he was circumcised on the eighth day after birth (Luke 2:21). It was a father's right to name his child and in this case too the heavenly Father had bestowed the name ('the name given by the angel before he was conceived in the womb,' 2:21). The name Jesus – in popular etymology, 'Yahweh saves' – suits perfectly the character of this Saviour revealed to the shepherds, he who is Christ the Lord. For, there is always the other side to this one like us. And, indeed, a purpose of the infancy gospels is to remind us of that 'other side'.

As one 'born under the law' Jesus was presented in the Temple forty days after birth (2:22-24). He accompanied his pious parents to Jerusalem for Passover (2:41-42). As a faithful Jewish boy he was obedient to his parents (2:51). Like any normal child, he developed physically and intellectually. The refrain of growth – 'The child grew and became strong, filled with wisdom; and the favour of God was upon him' (v. 40) – said of the baby being reared in his Nazareth home, is echoed in v. 52 when the twelve-year-old had returned to his home: 'And Jesus increased in wisdom and in years, and in divine and human favour.' Both sayings repeat in part what was said of the Baptist: 'The child grew and became strong in spirit' (1:80). The saying of 2:52 is practically a citation of 1 Sam 2:26 – 'Now the boy Samuel continued to grow both in stature and in favour with the Lord and with the people.'

Luke has carefully marked the physical development of Jesus: to *brephos* , 'the baby' (2:16), to *paidion*, 'the child'(v.40), *Iésous ho pais,* 'the boy Jesus' (v. 43), *Iésous* (v.52). In this latter verse we learn that his understanding also deepened and matured. The authentic humanity of Jesus demanded such growth in understanding. It also sets limits to his knowledge. Here scripture is formal (see Heb 2:17; 4:15; 5:7; Mk 13:32; 14:35-36). In short, Jesus would have blended with his Nazareth background. One can appreciate the amazed reaction when he first displayed his wisdom in his local synagogue: 'Is not this Joseph's son?!' (4:22).

The Jesus of Luke's infancy narrative is not, really, an anticipation of the Jesus of the ministry; instead, he reflects the Jesus of the ministry. The portrait of the baby is built out of what was known of his adult life. It was, rightly, discerned that what Jesus was seen to be during his ministry he had been from the very first. We may ask of the person and the role: what does he, himself, and what he stands for, mean for me here and now?

It seems to me that the finest christological statement is that of Paul: 'God was in Christ, reconciling the world to himself' (2 Cor 5:19). What a wealth of theology, and of soteriology, is there. Paul has told us where God is to be found: in Jesus of Nazareth, and why he is to be found in Jesus: to win humankind back to him. Where Jesus is, there is God. Logically, then, we have to find our God in a new-born babe. We are being challenged to see our God in one despised and rejected, in one tortured and hanging on a cross. A pious reading of the infancy gospels, leading to 'a gentle Jesus, meek and mild,' distorts the thrust of these stories. They are not 'romantic' stories because they are shot-through with the cross. And, if one does not discern the cross, and the incredible love of God it speaks, one will never know Emmanuel – 'God is with us' (Mt 1:23).

In the Lucan picture, manger and swaddling clothes, so domestic, an angelic choir, so heavenly, provide an idyllic touch. The acclaim of shepherds is poetic. But there is the disturbing word – the sign of contradiciton. There is the sword piercing the soul of the mother. The shadow of the cross falls across this story. It is not because our God is sadistic. It is because he is God of humankind, a God bent on the salvation of humankind. The suffering and death of Jesus confirm that not only death but suffering also may be common experience of friends of God. Suffering and death – least of all the suffering and death of his own Son – are not sought by God. Sadly, mysteriously, they are part of our human lot. Jesus – and the infancy narratives make plain that it was so from the beginning – was one who entered, wholly, into our human lot. In and through Jesus, God has assured us that he is the God who 'gave his only Son' (Jn 3:16-17; Rom 5:6-11). Paul can rightly ask: 'Will he not with him give us everything else?' (Rom 8:32).

CHAPTER 4

Prophet and Teacher

This is indeed the prophet who is to come into the world (Jn 6:14)

For you have one Teacher, the Christ (Mt 23:10)

The gospel tradition is fully assured that Jesus of Nazareth was prophet and teacher.[15] Luke casts him, firmly, in both roles. Here one looks at aspects of his presentation.

DECISION

Jesus, baptised by John, began his ministry as disciple of the Baptist. He went on to launch his own distinctive mission. This was a major decision which involved other decisions. He was thoroughly convinced of his calling. He had, however, to work out for himself how his mission would be carried through; he had to learn how, perfectly, to represent his Abba. To make the Abba known: that was his role. The temptation stories placed, dramatically, by Matthew and Luke before the opening of his mission, incorporate decisions he was to arrive at throughout his ministry.

Temptation (4:1-13)

Luke's temptation narrative is very close to that of Mt 4:1-11 except that he has inverted the order of the second and third temptations. Matthew's order – stones into bread, pinnacle of the temple, high mountain – is more logical. It cannot be doubted that Luke changed the order so that the series might end at Jerusalem. This is in keeping with his theological interest in the city. The three scenes serve to correct a false understanding of Jesus' mission as Son. They depict him as Son of God obedient to the Father's will, the faithful Son who will not be turned to invoking his authority for any other purpose than that for which he had been sent.

In each of his three ripostes to 'the devil' Jesus cited texts from Deuteronomy, and these texts are the key to the meaning of each scene. (1) 'One does not live by bread alone' (Deut 8:3). Jesus had been challenged miraculously to provide food for himself, to use his authority as Son apart from the Father's design. (2) 'Worship the Lord your God, and serve only him' (6:13). Jesus had been challenged to acknowledge someone other than the Father as Lord and Master. If he is to have *exousia*, authority, he will have it from the Father alone. He will learn that his exercise of authority will ever be in *diakonia*, service. (3) 'Do not put the Lord your God to the test' (6:16). Again, Jesus was challenged to use his power on his own behalf, this time to dazzle his contemporaries and conform to their image of a heaven-sent messiah. Each time Jesus had prevailed by 'the sword of the Spirit, which is the word of God' (Eph 6:17).

Jesus was 'tempted' in every resepct as we, yet without sinning (Heb 4:15). A consistent biblical pattern, representing God's respect for humankind, is the role of mediator in God's dealing with people. Jesus was mediator (Heb 5:1-3; 8:6). In keeping with the reality of the human situation, God saw it fitting that the Son who leads men and women to salvation should be made perfect through suffering (2:10). Jesus learned from his suffering what obedience to God's will meant for humankind – 'and having been made perfect he became the source of eternal salvation for all who obey him' (5:9). The temptations of Jesus are the ongoing temptations of Christians: to seek one's glory, even in religious matters; to seek the easy way and turn aside from suffering; to forget that the source of Christian life is to be found in the death and resurrection of Christ. Jesus redeemed humankind as the Suffering Servant and as Son of Man: by being one of us and in solidarity with his fellow men and women. We are redeemed by uniting ourselves with Christ. It is the way of countering the temptations that assail us.

THE PROGRAMME

Jesus knew it to be his vocation to proclaim the true God – the Father. He knew that in faithfulness to his task he was making the kingdom present – in other words, he was proclaiming the coming of God as salvation for humankind. How he saw his task is vividly portrayed in Luke's introduction to Jesus' ministry.

The Inauguration (4:14-30)

Coming to his Nazareth synagogue on a sabbath, Jesus was invited to take the scripture reading. He opened the scroll of Isaiah and read out:

The Spirit of the Lord is upon me,
because he has anointed me to bring good news to the poor.
He has sent me to proclaim release to the captives
and recovery of sight to the blind,
to let the oppressed go free,
to proclaim the year of the Lord's favour (Lk 4:18-19).

He had taken care to close his reading before the next phrase of the Isaian passage – 'and the day of vengeance of our God' (Is 61:2). 'Vengeance' would be no part of his message. Then he declared: 'Today this scripture has been fulfilled in your hearing' (Lk 4:21). The reaction of that Nazareth audience – his own people – was wonder and puzzlement. They think well of Jesus whom they know, they are lost in admiration of his gracious words – but can he, humble son of the humble Joseph, really apply to himself the text of Isaiah and put himself forward as a prophet? Most likely, the reply of Jesus (vv. 23-24) answered an objection raised by the people of Nazareth on a later visit – hence the reference to miracles at Capernaum (v. 23) which does not, obviously, fit the context of an inaugural appearance (as this purports to be).

In its current situation v. 23 – 'Do here also in your hometown the things that we have heard you did at Capernaum' – refers to a demand that Jesus should back his claim by miracles. V. 24 explains why he cannot do this: he shares the fate of every prophet – rejection by his own people. The passage, vv. 25-30, with its description of the people's violent reaction, really belongs at the close of the Galilean ministry (this passage is composite). Not accepted by his own people, Jesus, like his great prophetical predecessors, will find acceptance among Gentiles. The people rose in fury when they understood that the benefits they had rejected would be offered to the Gentiles (see Acts 13:46, 50). The ultimate fate of Jesus at the hands of his own people is foreshadowed, but his hour has not yet come (see Lk 9:51; Jn 7:30, 45; 8:59).

According to Deut 13:1-5, a false prophet was to be put to death. The citizens of Nazareth thought they had their man and were ready to carry out a threat once made against Jeremiah (Jer 11:12). But the Father has arranged the schedule for Jesus, and the time will come when there will be no escape (see Lk 20:15;

23:33); for Jesus committed the ultimate political gaffe of finding fault with his own people.[16]

The cycles of Elijah (1 Kgs 17-2 Kgs 1) and of Elisha (2 Kgs 2-13) witness to an acknowledgment of miracles as among the accomplishments of a prophet. All four gospels agree that Jesus worked miracles, in particular, miracles of healing.[17]

The Centurion's Servant (7:1-10)

The Sermon on the Plain (6:17-49) had been spoken in the hearing of Israel ('the people,' 7:1); it may be that in turning directly to the episode of the centurion, Luke wishes to foreshadow the Gentile mission. The story, indeed, may anticipate Acts 10:35 – 'in every nation anyone who fears him and does what is right is acceptable to him.' The centurion (certainly a Gentile, v. 5) may be an officer of Herod Antipas. He could also have been a Roman centurion in charge of a small outpost at Capernaum.

The centurion sent 'elders', distinguished members of the Jewish community of Capernaum, to Jesus. It was a service he could have made bold to ask of them and which they would have been glad to perform: 'he loves our people, and it is he who built our synagogue for us' (v. 5). He was, obviously, like Cornelius (Acts 10:1-2), a 'God-fearer', one of a class of Gentiles attracted to Judaism, but distinct from proselytes who took on full Jewish observance. These 'God-fearers' were freely admitted to synagogue worship; they came to know and appreciate the main tenets of the religion and to observe certain Jewish practices. The man was aware that Jesus, as a Jew, might be loth to incur the ritual defilement involved in entering a Gentile house (Lk 7:6-7; see Acts 10:28; 11:4); but his words, together with his action in sending an embassy rather than directly approaching Jesus, serve to emphasise the man's humility – a theme dear to Luke. The centurion (v. 8) was confident that Jesus can heal by word alone: as a soldier, and subject to authority himself, he knew how a word of command could bring results. Jesus' declaration (vv. 9-10) that the faith of this Gentile was greater than Israel's, prepares the reader for the later acceptance of the gospel by the Gentiles (see Acts 28:28).

A Widow's Son (7:11-17)

This is a passage peculiar to Luke who has inserted the miracle at this point in his gospel as a preparation for Jesus' reply to the Baptist ('the dead are raised.' v. 22). The added poignancy of a widow's only son moved Jesus to compassion. Here only is this sentiment attributed to him by Luke; but, indeed, the compassion of the Son of God is a major theme of the gospel. 'The Lord' (v. 13) henceforth, in Luke, appears regularly as a title of Jesus. It is a Christian title (see Rom 10:9; Phil 2:11) and Jesus was not addressed as 'Lord,' in this titular sense, during his ministry. *Kyrios* could, in its context, mean simply 'Sir.' The body of the young man, wrapped in a shroud, lay on a stretcher (not in a coffin); life was restored through the mere word of Jesus (vv. 14-15; compare 1 Kgs 17:19-22). Fear – 'Fear seized all of them' (v. 16) – is the normal reaction to a manifestation of divine power, quickly followed by praise of God. The people see in Jesus a great prophet, like Elijah or Elisha, who also raised from the dead (1 Kgs 17:17-24; 2 Kgs 4:18-37). The deed of Jesus represents a merciful intervention of God. In Jesus, God has indeed visited his people.

TEACHER

'He began to teach in their synagogues and was praised by everyone' (Lk 3:15). If Jesus were, undoubtedly, prophet, he stood too in the line of Old Testament wisdom teachers. Luke has frequent references to the teaching activity of Jesus. See 5:17; 6:6; 13:10, 22; 19:47; 20:1. Jesus was, by his opponents, regularly addressed as 'Teacher' (10:25; 11:45; 12:13; 20:28).

Sermon on the Plain (6:17-49)

Luke's Sermon (6:17-49), like Matthew's more elaborate Sermon on the Mount (Mt 5-7) is an *epitome:* a sophisticated digest of a longer work. Both Sermons group sayings of Jesus to serve as instructional material for Christians. In both, Jesus figures as a teacher addressing his disciples. Where Matthew develops the theme of the Two Ways (see Deut 11:26-30; 30:15-20) Luke contrasts two types of person, 'the good person' and 'the bad' (Lk 6:45). These are, equivalently, 'the rich' and 'the poor' (6:20b-26). The two *epitomai* are creations of the Jesus-movement: the one to instruct converts from Judaism (Matthew), to other to instruct those coming from a

Hellenistic background (Luke).[18] One assumes that each evangelist had adapted the source.

After an introduction and an exordium (beatitudes and woes, 6:17-26), Luke's Sermon falls into two parts: the conduct of disciples toward the outside world (vv. 27-38) and within the community (vv. 39-45). The basis of the whole is Jesus' love-command: 'Love your enemies, do good to those who hate you. Bless those who curse you, pray for those who abuse you' (vv. 27b-28). This is followed by four examples of how the maxims should be understood (vv. 29-30). The Golden Rule – 'do to others as you would have them do to you' (v. 31) – proposes a basic ethical principle. The verses 32-35 set out some of the implications of its implementation. The exhortation, 'Be merciful, just as your Father is merciful' (v. 36), leads to the practical applications of vv. 37-38 which warn against a judgmental attitude and stress forgiveness. Behind all stands, evidently, an image of a gracious and forgiving God.

There are three basic rules for conduct within the community: relationship between student and teacher – 'everyone who is fully qualified will be like the teacher' (v. 40); relationships between students – to remove the log from one's own eye before searching out the speck in another's (vv. 41-42); relationship towards oneself – rightly to evaluate oneself (vv. 43-45). The conclusion (vv. 47-49) is an admonition on hearing and doing 'my words'. The ultimate criterion is no longer the Law but the living words of the Lord. And not hearing only but doing as well – orthopraxis. A familiar parable offers an unambiguous illustration.

The Good Samaritan (10:25-37)

The introduction (10:25-29) is essential for an understanding of the Good Samaritan. The lawyer's question – 'What must I do to inherit eternal life? – was meant to embarrass Jesus; he, adroitly, put the onus on his questioner, who found that his reply (from Deut 6:5 and Lev 19:18) won the approval of Jesus. The lawyer tried again and asked for a definition of 'neighbour'. This time he felt that the 'Master' would be hard put to counter for he had raised what was, in fact, a much disputed matter. The Essenes of Qumran, for instance, would maintain that all 'sons of darkness', that is, all who did not belong to the sect, should be excluded. Others, while less radical, would rule out 'sinners'. All would agree that, in the broadest interpretation, 'neighbour' should be limited to Jews and proselytes. It is expected that Jesus, too, will respect the broad limits. It remains to be seen whether he will narrow them appreciably.

Though not explicitly stated, it is certainly implied that the man who was mugged on the road to Jericho was a Jew (v. 30). His nationality is not expressly mentioned because the point of the parable is that the lawyer's question is not going to be answered in terms of nationality or race. Priest and Levite refused to become involved in what, one way or other, was sure to be a messy business (vv. 31-33). Jesus did not accuse them of callousness, he did not pass judgment on their conduct. They were men who lacked the courage to love; dare we say that they represent the common man? After priest and Levite it might have been expected that the third traveller – a series of three is typical of story – would turn out to be a Jewish layman; the bias would be anticlerical. The drama is that the third character, the hero of the story, was one of the despised Samaritans. He has been designedly chosen to bring out the unselfishness of love. The man applied first-aid to the wounded traveller and carried him to an inn; and he did not consider that his obligations had thereby ended. Whatever a cynic might have thought of his conduct so far, the man turns out to be very much the realist. He did not naïvely presume on the softheartedness of the innkeeper but paid him, in advance, to look after the victim.

At the close, Jesus got the lawyer to answer his own question — 'The one who showed him mercy' (v. 37). Yet, had he really responded to the original question? In v. 29 he had asked: 'Who is my neighbour?', while the question that Jesus put to him in v. 36 is rather: 'To whom am I neighbour?' The lawyer was concerned with the object of love and his question implied a limitation: my neighbour is one who belongs to such and such a group. Jesus looked to the subject of love: which of the three had acted as neighbour? The lawyer's question was not answered because it was a mistaken question. One cannot determine theoretically who one's neighbour is because love is not theory but practice. One's neighbour is any person who needs one's help, says the parable. The wounded man was neighbour to the priest and Levite just as much as he was to the Samaritan, but while they had theorised in the manner of the lawyer, he had acted. The traveller was neighbour to all three; the Samaritan alone was neighbour in return. The lawyer had, seemingly, learned his lesson. At least he had answered correctly: 'The one who showed him mercy.' But he could not bring himself to say, simply: the Samaritan.

Though the recommendation of Jesus – 'Go, and do likewise' (v. 37) – was addressed to the lawyer it holds a message and a warning for all Christians. We may not pause to ask ourselves: 'Is this person really my neigbour?' Christian charity knows no bounds. The pity is that there are so few 'Samaritans' among us.

Martha and Mary (10:38-42)

On his journey to Jerusalem, Jesus 'entered a certain village' (10:38). From John 11:1 we learn that the village was Bethany, on the eastern slope of the Mount of Olives. Here is an instance of the elasticity of Luke's 'journey'; in 17:11 Jesus will still be at 'the region between Samaria and Galilee'. In John 11:1-44 the sisters Martha and Mary have the same contrasting temperaments as in Luke's narrative. The familiar relationship betwen Jesus and the women, explicitly remarked in John 11:5 – 'Jesus loved Martha and her sister' – is here graphically portrayed: an exasperated Martha does not hesitate to point out that it is Jesus' fault that she had been left on her own to make all the preparations (Lk 10:40). He gently chided her for her agitation (v. 41). There is textual confusion with regard to v. 42a. The longer reading, impressively attested ('few things are necessary or only one') refers to the needless concern of Martha – one dish will suffice. The shorter reading ('there is need of only one thing') may well be authentic: Martha is told that the one thing necessary is the presence of the Lord and the word which he imparts. He, indeed, is host rather than guest. Mary, drinking in the words of the Lord (v. 39), is displaying 'undivided devotion to the Lord' (1 Cor 7:35).

The story has to do with a Christian community situation. Jesus is *ho kyrios* throughout: Lord and Teacher. Martha is typical of a class of women who figure in Luke-Acts: relatively well-off women ('Martha welcomed him into her home,' Lk 10:38) who were generous to the community or to itinerant preachers (see Lk 8:1-3; Acts 9:36-39; 16:15, 40). Here the role of Martha is contrasted with that of

Mary: a disciple sitting at the feet of the Lord and listening to his word (Luke 10:39a). The notable feature is the depiction of a woman as student of the word and the Lord's emphatic approval of the role. There was little problem about the 'diaconal' role of women in the early church. In contrast, their active role in ministry, well attested in the Pauline letters, soon became problematic – witness 1 Timothy. There was a backlash, following on the choice of patriarchy as the model of church authority (see 1 Tim 3:1-13; 2:8-15). The place of Mary in Lk 10 is in tension with his subordinate role of women throughout Acts.[19] He has, yet again, acknowledged an earlier tradition. 'Mary has chosen the better part' (10:42) – Martha's part is good too. The immediately preceding parable of the Good Samaritan underlines the essential place of loving service.

SUFFERING PROPHET

'Was it not necessary that the Messiah should suffer these things and so enter into his glory?' (Lk 24:26). This is the reaction of the Risen Lord to the consternation of the Emmaus disciples. Jesus of Nazareth, 'a prophet mighty in deed and word' (v.19), had been condemned to death and crucified. Suffering is an inescapable feature of the role of the Messiah.

Suffering Prophet (9:18-24)

Luke gives no indication of the setting of Peter's confession (9:18-20). He has deliberately avoided mentioning Caesarea Philippi (Mk 8:27) lest it distract from the central place of Jerusalem in his gospel and also because Galilee is the scene of the first part of Jesus' mission. Typically (Lk 9:18-19), Luke refers to the prayer of Jesus: 'Once when Jesus was praying alone, with only the disciples near him' (9:18; see 3:21; 5:16; 6:12). Even after the multiplication of loaves people still think of Jesus in the same manner as before (v. 19 – as John the Baptist, Elijah, or a former prophet); mark the rumours which Herod Antipas had heard (9:7-8). Luke here provides the answer to Jesus' identity. He is 'The Messiah of God' (v. 20): God's solemnly designated envoy. Luke (v. 22) has omitted the intervention of Peter and Jesus' rebuke of him (Mk 8:32-33). In Mark's gospel, Peter's profession, followed by the prediction of the passion (8:27-33), signals a turning point: the public ministry is over. Jesus goes to his death. In Luke's plan the ministry continues.

Jesus' messiahship involves suffering, repudiation and death (Lk 8:22). A word to the disciples (v. 18) now opens out into an invitation to all: 'If any want to become my followers, let them deny themselves and take up their cross daily and follow me'(v. 23). Three conditions are listed: denying oneself, that is to say, not being preoccupied with oneself and one's selfish interests but having in mind him whose disciple one would be; taking up one's cross by patiently bearing trials and so dying to the world (see 1 Cor 15:31) – the 'daily' taking up of the cross is a broadening of a saying of Jesus which originally pointed to martyrdom (see Mk 8:34). These later conditions really prepare the way for the first: the following of Jesus by embracing his way of life (9:23-25).

The emergence of the prophet Jesus marks a time of decision, a crisis in which no one can be neutral (12:49-53). The verses 49-50 – 'I came to bring fire to the earth, and how I wish it were kindled. I have a baptism with which to be baptised, and what stress I am under until it is completed!' – proper to Luke, may, at one level, be considered independently of their context. The fire which Jesus wished to see kindled is that which purifies, a fire lighted on the cross (see Jn 12:32). The 'baptism' is the Passion which will 'plunge' Jesus into a sea of suffering. Jesus was bringer of salvation to humankind but he was aware that the way to salvation was through suffering – through fire and water (see Lk 24:41-44). Luke, however, has understood the saying of 12:49-50 in relation to vv. 51-53, on peace or division. The description of family dissension (dramatic presentation of the division he occasions) is based on Mic 7:6. In this passage of Luke we discern another Johannine contact because a feature of the fourth gospel, met with again and again, is that Christ, by his very presence, brings *krisis* or 'judgment': people must be for or against the light (see Jn 8:12; chapter 9).

Peter, in reply to Jesus' question, declared Jesus to be 'the Messiah of God' (9:20). Jesus then proclaimed his understanding of messiahship by stressing suffering and death (v. 22). The transfiguration which followed (9:28-36) confirmed the last part of the announcement: 'and on the last day be raised' (compare the 'and then enter into his glory' of 24:26). Peter misunderstood. The three booths he suggested – one each for Jesus, Moses and Elijah – would have all three on an equal footing. Peter really 'did not know what he said' (v. 33).

The voice from heaven set the record straight: 'This is my Son, my chosen' (v. 35). Jesus is not a Moses nor an Elijah *redivivus* – he is uniquely God's Son (see Heb 3:1-6). 'Listen to him': this Son is the eschatological Prophet who has spoken God's definitive word. Luke tells us that Moses and Elijah, representatives of the Old Testament, had spoken with Jesus of his *exodos* (his exit, his passing, his departure) which he was to accomplish in Jerusalem. His 'exodus' was his death, his passing to the Father, which would be the new exodus of salvation for Christians. Furthermore, the three privileged disciples 'saw his glory'; not yet a vision of resurrection glory but an anticipated glimpse of it. The transfiguration episode took on significance when the disciples looked back on it in the light of the resurrection. It helped them to realise that the glory of the risen Lord had been hiddenly present in Jesus of Nazareth.

DISCIPLESHIP

A look at Jesus' expectation of disciples, and at their response, will give some insight into the character of the Prophet/Teacher.

Let the Dead Bury Their Dead (9:57-62)

At the start of Luke's travel account (9:51-18:14), when Jesus 'set his face to go to Jerusalem' (9:51), the passage 9:57-62 introduces three would-be followers of Jesus. In response to one who declares that he is prepared to follow Jesus anywhere the point is made that the disciple of Jesus must be, like him, a homeless wanderer: 'Foxes have holes, and birds of the air have nests; but the Son of Man has nowhere to lay his head' (v. 58). In vv. 59-60 an aspiring disciple asserts that he must wait until his father has died before he can go with Jesus – he invokes the fourth commandment. He is told that others who are 'dead', not challenged by this call of Jesus, will take care of the man's obligations. Luke adds the commission: 'Go and proclaim the kingdom of God.' Discipleship implies the proclamation of the word. Like Elisha (1 Kgs 19:19-21) the third man (Lk 9:61-62) wants to take leave of his family. Jesus is more demanding than Elijah (who had granted Elisha leave to make his farewell). One must here, as frequently in the gospels, be sensitive to the Semitic penchant for expression in an extreme form as a means of emphasis. Jesus' pronouncement, in proverbial form, should be understood in the same manner: 'No one who puts a hand to the plough and looks back is fit for the kingdom of God' (v. 62). A preacher of the kingdom will have the forthrightness of a ploughman who gives his whole attention to ploughing a straight furrow.

The sayings declare, in forthright language, that sacrifice and self-commitment are expected of a disciple of Jesus. They suggest, too, that life's most painful choices are not between good and evil but between the good and the better way. The quality of discipleship set forth in this passage is prompted by the example of the Prophet who walks resolutely towards the goal (51:1).

The Seventy (10:1-20)

The passage 10:1-16 is parallel to 9:1-6 (the mission of the Twelve). It does not seem that this sending of the seventy foreshadows, as has been suggested, the universal mission of Jesus' disciples; in 14:47 the Gentile mission is entrusted to the Twelve. The role of the seventy is not that of the messengers of 9:52 (sent, unsuccessfully, to prepare his visit to a Samaritan village); it is a preaching mission. Two, obviously distinct, sayings follow: 'The harvest is plentiful, but the labourers are few; therefore ask the Lord of the harvest to send out labourers into his harvest. Go on your way. See, I am sending you out like lambs into the midst of wolves' (vv. 2- 3). Taken together, they expresss the experience of the first missionaries: their own zeal and the opposition they encountered. The warning (v. 4) not to waste time on civilities (elaborate, in the oriental manner) underlines the urgency of the mission. 'Peace' (shalom) is the Jewish greeting. One who 'shares in peace' is, literally, 'son of peace' – one worthy of peace. Clearly, the greeting is meaningful, a blessing. Food and shelter (v. 7) are not alms but wages (see 1 Cor 9:14).

The mission was not a private sally but a proclamation of the kingdom. The kingdom is near, so they are not to waste time on those who will not receive them; the message must be brought to others (vv. 10-11). 'Whoever listens to you listens to me' (v. 16): Jesus, sent by the Father, has sent the disciples. Acceptance or rejection of them is acceptance or rejection of God. As for the disciples, not missionary success but assurance of being numbered among the elect – 'your names are written in heaven' – is the ultimate reason for rejoicing (v. 20). See Rev 3:5; 13:8; 17;8; 20:12,15.

Counting the Cost (14:25-33)

The twin parables of Tower-builder and King (14:28-32) drive home the lesson that discipleship does demand commitment; it cannot be undertaken casually. Though the parables seem repetitive they are, in fact, complementary. In the first, the builder was free to undertake his construction or not; he was considering the matter in the abstract. The king, on the other hand, was already up against it: his country had been invaded (the other king was 'advancing against him'); therefore he had to act. There are two factors in the call to follow Christ: We have to count the cost both of accepting that invitation and of rejecting it. One who comes to Christ must come with eyes wide open.

The parables may seem discouraging but they are to be understood in much the same manner as the saying of v. 26 – on 'hating' family: an emphatic statement of commitment. The following of Christ is at all times a serious business and, in certain circumstances, it can be a very serious business indeed. This is so, for instance, in time of persecution. It is scarcely less true in the modern world where the Christian is called upon to renounce much that is taken for granted by others. If one does walk after the Master one must be prepared to take up one's cross (v. 27). One cannot, without fault, shirk one's obligations as a Christian. The encouraging factor is that the Christ who calls does know the cost involved and knows, too, human frailty, and will lavish his grace on one who really strives to answer his call. V. 33 – 'So therefore, none of you can become my disciple if you do not give up all your possessions' – is a practical consequence of the parables rather than their moral. The 'all' emphasis is typically Lucan. Jesus had envisaged discipleship as comprising both a core, totally committed group, and a broader membership. In Acts, Luke acknowledges this situation.

Worthless Servants (17:7-10)

The parable of the Worthless Servants (17:7-10) is one which would have shocked Jesus' hearers not because of the use of the term *doulos* ('slave') but because of the manner in which this servanthood is to be lived before God. The picture he has painted is starkly clear. A slave has no claim on his master – neither wages nor thanks – independently of how much he may have done for his master. His service is utterly taken for granted. The application of the parable: 'So you also, when you have done all that you were ordered to do, say, "We are worthless slaves; we have done only what we ought to have done!"'(v. 10) strikes at the roots of an ethical attitude of some at least in contemporary Judaism. In their religious consciousness, God 'owed' humans salvation in view of the just person's fidelity to the Law. But Jesus sets a person in *direct* relationship to God, that is, without the Law intervening. He establishes a person as a *doulos* over against God, standing in obedience to the personal and acknowledged sovereignty of God. There is no doubt that the parable belongs to Jesus' criticism of the theology of his contemporaries: he pronounced a radically negative verdict on the idea of reward. What he does acknowledge is something quite different: the reality of divine recompense, of God's sheer generosity.

Luke began chapter 17 with the phrase, 'He said to his disciples'; then, in v. 5, the apostles (the inner group) ask for an increase in faith, and the parable is addressed to them. It would appear, then, that Luke has especially in mind the missioners or itinerant preachers of the gospel. They are reminded of the attitude they ought to have: the consciousness of serving without claim or reward. Paul had understood: 'I planted, Apollos watered, but God gave the growth. So neither the one who plants nor the one who waters is anything, but only God who gives the growth' (1 Cor 3:6-7). This attitude must, inevitably, colour the relationship of ministers of the word to those whom they serve in the Lord. The Son of Man had come 'not to be served, but to serve' (Mk 10:45). His servants, too, must find their *exousia*, authority, in *diakonia*, service.

Those Who Humble Themselves (14:7-11)

In Lk 14:1-24 four episodes are set in the context of a meal, hosted by a Pharisee (14:1). Luke gives the impression that Jesus was indeed not infrequently a guest of Pharisees. This is really not surprising because, despite their serious differences, Jesus and the Pharisees had much in common. He could dialogue with them, something that was not feasible with the Temple priests. At first sight, vv. 7-11 seem to offer a lesson in etiquette. Luke, however, calls the passage a 'parable'. Later on the scribes – effectively, the theologians – are characterised as those who 'love the places of honour at banquets' (20:46). In our text, such conduct, presented in parabolic guise, is censured and made the object of a warning. One who had seated himself 'at the place of honour' must yield to the eminent guest for whom the place had been reserved. Because, in the meantime, the intermediary places will have been filled, he must take the lowest place (vv. 7-9). For v. 10 compare Proverbs 25:7 – 'It is better to be told "come up here" than to be put lower in the presence of a noble.' The key to the passage is v. 11, a saying which occurs, too, in 18:14 as a generalising conclusion to the Pharisee and the Publican: 'For all who exalt themselves will be humbled, and those who humble themselves will be exalted.' It is more at home here. The passive stands for divine action: God will humble or exalt.

We are carried beyond the perspective of human relationships and assured that God is no respecter of persons. Now the drift of the parable becomes clear. If the scribes and Pharisees had arrogated to themselves privileges and expected preferential treatment, they did so on the ground of their observance of the Law, on their standing as religious people. They took for granted that God would see things in this light and extend to them preferential treatment (see 18:9-14). Here they are firmly warned that they may be fortunate to scrape into the banquet. It is not difficult to see that the warning might, with reason, if not with profit, have sounded down the centuries, and could continue to ring in the ears of the professional religious of the Christian church.

CONCLUSION

Jesus of Nazareth was a prophet. A prophet is God's spokesperson. As one who spoke God's definitive word (see Heb 1:2), he was the eschatological prophet. As 'image of the invisible God' (Col 1:15) everything he did and said was manifestation of God. Jesus served his prophetical apprenticeship under John the Baptist. His decision to launch his distinctive mission was based on his consciousness of a unique relationship with his Abba. He knew himself to be one called and sent: 'I must proclaim the good news of the kingdom of God ... for I was sent for this purpose' (Lk 4:43). The rule of God is, in the long run, God himself as salvation of humankind. Salvation reaches into every area of human life. As with Elijah and Elisha, healing was part of Jesus' prophetic mission. This is explicit in his inaugural programme (4:14-30).

In Jesus, the roles of prophet and teacher overlapped. If he was in the tradition of the prophets of Israel, he was also in the tradition of the sages of Israel. He transcended their role also. They were persuasive. He displayed another quality: 'They were astounded at his teaching, because he spoke with authority' (4:31). Another quality indeed, because his *exousia* carried no trace of domineering. He could tell his disciples: 'I am among you as one who serves' (22:26). The authority of his teaching lay in the fact that his words were healing words, saving words. He would exhort his disciples: 'Be merciful, just as your Father is merciful' (6:36). As teacher and prophet, he had disciples: men and women followed him. He sought to form them. He was particulary concerned with those who were called to follow him wholly. Such must not fail to respond, but should do so in awareness of what was being asked of them. They should know that their Master was a Prophet who had been rejected and had suffered. The disciple is not greater than the master. At the end of all they must be clear that there is no place for self-congratulation. Their faithful service *is* their reward. Jesus' faithful service was *his* reward. There is consolation in the assurance that a generous God rejoices in their service as he rejoiced in the loving service of the Son.

Jesus' understanding of discipleship was broader. Not all – in truth, only a few – are summoned to leave everything and follow. Martha and Mary were not in his entourage. And Zacchaeus, though radically changed, stayed on in his job (19:1-10). But, now, he was living witness, proclaiming a word of hope: the Son of Man had come to seek out and save the lost (v. 10).

CHAPTER 5

Vindicator of the Poor

Since there will never cease to be some in need on the earth, I therefore command you, 'Open your hand to the poor and needy neighbour in your land' (Deut 15:11).

Jesus had a free attitude to property. Himself of 'lower middle-class' Galilean background – he was a *tektón*, an artisan (Mk 6:3) – he took for granted the owning of property.

When he began his ministry and had abandoned his trade, he was supported, in his itinerant mission, by well-to-do women disciples (Lk 8:2-3). He urged that parents must be supported from their children's' means (Mk 7:9-10) and recommended that possessions be used to help the needy (12:41-42). In requiring money to be lent without hope of return (Mt 5:42), Jesus was presupposing surplus funds that could be lent. The chief tax-collector Zacchaeus was ready to give half his possessions to the poor (Lk 10:8-9). Jesus was invited to dinner by the rich and privileged (Lk 7:36; 14:1,12). In the parable of the Labourers in the Vineyard he has the employer declare: 'Am I not allowed to do what I choose with what belongs to me?' (Mt 20:15). While all of this may not, as such, go back in detail to Jesus himself, there is a pattern that surely reflects his attitude.

On the other hand, Jesus himself, during his itinerant mission, had no possessions. And he did, with severity, attack wealth where it had captured people's hearts and had blinded their eyes to God's purpose. He had especially in mind surplus wealth: the rich ought to use their wealth to benefit the poor. An aspect of the camel saying – 'It is easier for a camel to go through the eye of a needle than for someone who is rich to enter the kingdom of God' (Mk 10:25, parr.) – is that it expresses the real difficulty the rich have in freeing themselves of possessiveness.

All the while, the call of Jesus to the following of him in discipleship was to a following then and there. He thought and spoke of the kingdom not only in future terms but, also, as a present reality. We have, for instance, the sayings: 'If it is by the finger of God that I cast out demons, then the kingdom of God has come to you' (Lk 1:20) and 'the kingdom of God is among you' (17:21). The kingdom – better, the reign or rule – of God is not primarily a state or place but rather the dynamic event of God coming in power to rule his people Israel in the end-time. For Jesus the rule of God – God as salvation for humankind – has to be a reality among men and women on earth already in the here and now. He was making God's gracious power present not only in his healings and overcoming of evil but, also, in his concern for the poor. God's rule becomes real when it finds expression in human life. It found expression in the life of Jesus. he 'went about, doing good'; he championed the outcast, he welcomed and pardoned sinners. Jesus, in his own lifestyle, gave concrete expression to the good life – a life worthy of humankind. He demonstrated that the kingdom is a reality of this world. It is our task to give it shape in our world.

The Poor

Jesus knew it to be his vocation to proclaim the true God – the Father. He knew that in faithfulness to his task he was making the kingdom present. How he saw his task is vividly portrayed in Luke's introduction of Jesus' ministry in 4:16-21.[20] In his programmatic statement, Jesus pointed to the recipients of his good news: captives, blind, oppressed – all who are weakest and powerless. They are 'the poor'.

The 'poor' are not only those with few or no possessions, and not only those whose poverty is 'spiritual'. In the biblical context the poor are the 'little people' who are incapable of standing up for themselves and hence, by reason of their need and sorry state, are God's protected ones. The designation 'poor' (as in Luke's beatitudes, for instance) is not idealisation: the poor really do need help, the hungry stand in need of nourishment, the mourning are visibly sorrowing. All cry out for compassion. The 'poor' to whom Jesus announced the good news of the kingdom and whom he pronounced 'blessed' are not those whom he proposed as models of virtue but are persons literally 'down and out'. The kingdom of

God, the consolation of the new age, is granted to the weak and despised – to those who suffer, who weep, who sorrow.

The Beatitudes (6:20-26)

Our gospels have two, notably different, versions of the beatitudes: Mt 5:3-12 and Lk 6:20-23. Matthew has nine beatitudes. Luke has four – but with corresponding 'woes' (Lk 6:24-26). Both versions have grown from an original core going back to Jesus, the additions and adaptations being due to the evangelists (or the traditions they had inherited). We can, without much trouble, discern a form of the beatitudes which would stand as a common basis for the development of the evangelists and which may reasonably be regarded as representing the beatitudes of Jesus. These are three:

> Blessed are the poor, for the kingdom is theirs.
> Blessed are those who hunger, for they will be filled.
> Blessed are the afflicted, for they will be comforted.

The beatitudes do not refer to three different categories but to three aspects of the same distressful situation. The first sets the tone. In declaring the poor blessed, Jesus gives concrete expression to the good news which he brings to the poor. The other two beatitudes make precise, and develop, the content of the first. In the gospels, the poor are the indigent, those who depend totally on alms – they are the hungry, those who grieve over their unhappy lot. The most important text of the earliest Jesus tradition is this beatitude addressed to the poor. It is a fulfilment of Is 61:1 – 'He has sent me to bring good news to the oppressed' – a promise that the wretched lot of the poor will be reversed under the reign of God. In Palestine, poor Jews were coming together as followers of Jesus. Their present experience of poverty, hunger and tears played a decisive part in determining the object of their hope: they firmly expected that their lot would be reversed (see Lk 1:52-53). Jesus was hope of the poor.

Luke and Matthew have in common the three beatitudes of Jesus. They have in common a fourth: the blessedness of those who suffer persecution for the sake of Christ. This was, likely, added in the tradition but, for practical purposes, we may regard it as a beatitude of Luke (6:22-23). In Luke's vision this standpoint of the beatitude of the persecuted because of Christ is extended to the previous beatitudes (vv. 20-21) which now also directly call to Christian readers.

Jesus had spoken to the poor as such, the afflicted and the hungry; their very distress was enough to make them privileged before God. By Luke the beatitudes are now addressed to poor Christians. The promised blessedness will wonderfully compensate them for their present privations. But they ultimately owe their blessedness to their status as disciples of Christ.

In Luke's vocabulary – 'Blessed are you who are poor, for yours is the kingdom of God' (6:20) – the *ptóchoi*, 'poor,' are the indigent, people who lack the necessities of life. The 'hungry' – 'Blessed are you who are hungry now, for you will be filled' (6:21a) – are the poor regarded in the concrete circumstances of their lives; they have no food. In contrast, the 'rich' – 'But woe to you who are rich, for you have received your consolation' (6:24) – are those whose wealth insulates them from concern for those in need; they are sheltered from misery, the lot of the poor. The 'full' – 'Woe to you who are full now, for you will be hungry' (6:25) – are people who have everything. These terms illustrate the realism of Luke's assessment of the respective situations of rich and poor. Deprived of material goods and, by themselves, unable to obtain these goods, the poor go homeless and hungry, while the rich can gratify their desires.

The 'laughter' – 'Blessed are you who weep now, for you will laugh' – of the third woe expresses the satisfied wellbeing of the fortunate ones of the world. The 'tears' – 'Blessed are you who weep now, for you will laugh' – of the third beatitude expresses the distress of those who know in their world privation and suffering. The beatitude is addressed to unhappy people, crushed by their circumstances. Again, in the fourth woe, the 'flattered' – 'Woe to you when all speak well fo you, for this is what their ancestors did to the false prophets' (6:26) – are the 'beautiful people' while the 'reviled' – 'Blessed are you when people hate you, and when they exclude you, revile you and defame you on account of the Son of Man' (6:22) – are suffering and persecuted Christians. Luke fixed his attention on the implication of the beatitudes: they clarify the mission of Jesus, the role of Saviour which he is called upon to exercise in favour of those who believe in him, especially in favour of those who suffer for their faith in him. These beatitudes now apply to the real conditions of Christian disciples as Luke discerns them.

GREED – COVETOUSNESS (*Pleonexia*)

Jesus spoke the parable of the Rich Fool (12:16-21) in response to the threat of *pleonexia* – 'Take care! Be on your guard against all kinds of greed' (v. 15). In Hellenistic ethics *pleonexia*, 'greed', 'covetousness', was emphatically viewed as a serious disorder. Along this line one might regard the rich farmer of the parable as a social sinner, carried away by greed. By storing up grain he had harmed society; holding back his produce would drive up the price of grain. The death of the speculator occurs at the very moment when he believes he can at last rest from his frenetic pursuit of profit. Luke, however, may not have thought along those lines. He is more concerned with the man's shortsightedness.

The request by 'someone in the crowd' for a ruling in a matter of inheritance (v.13), occasioning a warning against greed or cupidity (v.15), constitutes the setting of the Rich Fool. The parable illustrates the peril to which 'greed' exposes one. In v. 21, conclusion of the parable, Luke spoke his basic verdict: 'So it is with those who store up treasures for themselves but are not rich toward God.' The man had failed to take the positive ethical steps which a rich Christian must take to be saved. Jesus went on (12:22-24) to outline his demands on disciples and to sketch their corresponding lifestyle, wholly at odds with that of the rich man.

In Luke's eyes the error of the rich man lay, positively, in having thought only of his 'soul' – his self-centredness. He had stored up his harvest in view of having a good time for the rest of his life (12:19). His attitude might well be that of the discontented heir (v.13; see 15:12-13). It corresponded to the outlook of people who are preoccupied with where to dine and what to wear (v. 22). It was the attitude of pagans (v. 30). The error of the unhappy man comprised three factors: forgetfulness of God, forgetfulness of eternal life, forgetfulness of his obligation to the poor. He was truly a 'fool' because he had not known how to use wisely the wealth he enjoyed.

The parable of the Rich Fool, which warns against the tendency to seek security in wealth (12:15-21) should not be taken in isolation from the following development (vv. 22-24). Here, addressing his *disciples* (v.22), Jesus put them on their guard, not against the danger of wealth (no immediate threat to them) but simply against the normal anxiety of the poor, that for basic needs. In dreaming of his full barns, the rich man had a sense of *security* (v.19). The disciples, who possess nothing, vividly feel their insecurity (vv. 22, 29). There is no question of condemning a longing for security inherent in the human condition. Rather, the intention is to show that the need goes astray when it seeks its sole support in earthly resources. There is no authentic security that is not founded on God, on a vivid consciousness of his parently solicitude. A measure of that trust is the radical challenge: 'Sell your possessions, and give alms' (v. 33).

Again, one notes that there is no suggestion that wealth is evil in itself, independently of the disposition it may engender. Wealth is misfortune when it not only makes one indifferent to the good of the future life and when it distracts the rich from concern for the poor. It also tends to foster in the rich a feeling of security which is incompatible with that trust which God claims for himself alone. In contrast, a 'little flock' in a hostile world, disciples should not be discouraged but should look in trust to a Father who has chosen them for his kingdom (v. 32). In v. 3 Luke has rewritten a saying that may, originally, have been close to Matthew's version (Mt 6:20-21); the threat of riches and the value of almsgiving are favourite themes of Luke. The closing admonition puts the matter in a nutshell: 'Where your treasure is, there your heart will be also' (v. 34). If the heart is set on the kingdom (v. 31) then one will have the right perspective.

The Astute Manager (16:1-8 [9-13])

The parable of the Astute Manager (Lk 16:1-8) was one which Jesus' hearers would have appreciated. They would have enjoyed the humour of his bold characterisation: his putting forward of a rascal as a spur to resolute decision and action. The manager (steward) had been accused of embezzlement. Until he produced his books he had a breathing-space. He rewrote contracts – in favour of his master's creditors and in view of a kickback. It was a neat scam! The master, who had to honour the contracts duly made in his name, ruefully applauded the resourceful conduct of his unscrupulous manager. Jesus would wish that his disciples show as much resourcefulness in God's business as men of the world do in their affairs.

Outside of Palestine (and the Jewish legal system) the parable quickly raised the problem of how this unprincipled rascal could be, in any sense, an example. The verses 10-13 are meant to answer the question prompted by the manager's conduct. He is no longer an example but a warning. It is noteworthy that these additions leave the substance of the parable unchanged; they do bear witness to an interpretation of a parable which was now applied by the early church to the community. It was, however, an application in line with the parable. The resolute action which Jesus recommended does embrace the generosity of v. 9, the faithfulness of vv. 10-11 and the rejection of mammon in v. 13. Christians, in applying this parable to themselves, had caused a shift of emphasis. They were able to bring its teaching to bear on their daily lives because they lived in the atmosphere of the decision it urgently enjoined: they had embraced the kingdom.

Luke is more precise. In vv. 1-9 the crafty manager is brought forward to teach Christians the wise use of money: to make friends with it so that at death, when money fails, their friends can welcome their benefactors into eternal dwellings. To use money wisely is to give it the poor and thus ensure one's eternal lot. The woe of the rich is linked to the horizon on which their eyes are fixed: 'where your treasure is, there your heart will be also' (11:34). And even if the rich hear the word, 'they are choked by the cares and riches and pleasures of life, and their fruit does not mature' (8:14); their hearts are 'weighed down with dissipation and drunkenness and the worries of this life' (21:34). They become incapable of looking beyond the present life. Such is the conviction of Luke. He, obviously, had to do with a community in which many were prosperous.

The parable of the Astute Manager says in positive terms what the parable of the Rich Fool (12:3-21) says negatively. The manager was, at least, astute: his example (in Christian reinterpretation) teaches people to use their earthly goods in view of heavenly reward. Just as the 'woes' (6:24-26) were addressed to the rich, the episode of the 'ruler' illustrates the extreme difficulty a rich person faces in finding salvation (18:18-27). The case of Zacchaeus shows that an exception is always possible. Jesus declared of him: 'Today salvation has come to this house' (19:9). But in Luke's narrrative this verdict is firmly linked to the resolve of the rich tax-collector: 'Look, half of my possessions, Lord, I will give to the poor; and if I have defrauded anyone of anything, I will pay back four times as much' (v. 8; see Ex 22:1). Zacchaeus is saved but his fortune has gone back to the poor and to those who had been victims of his exactions. Inexorably, Luke maintains his position that the proper use of wealth is to distribute it to the poor.

Luke calls the Pharisees money-lovers: 'The Pharisees, who were lovers of money, scoffed at him' (16:14). *Philargyria* is love of money, it is avarice. We are reminded of the familiar text: 'For the love of money is the root of all evil' (1 Tim 6:1). Far from being singular, this was, in one form or other, a saying common in the Hellenistic world. For example, Strobaeus: 'Bion the sophist used to say that money is the mother-city *(métropolis)* of all evil' (Eccl 3). And Polycarp: 'But the beginning of all evils is the love of money' (Phil 4:1). A wry acknowledgment that wealth has its problems.

Even though these sayings of Lk 16:9-13 are complementary to the parable of the Astute Manager, it is not unfair to say that the ultimate message of the parable, as Luke understands it, is given in v. 13 – 'No slave can serve two masters; for a slave will either hate the one and love the other, or be devoted to the one and despise the other. You cannot serve God and wealth [mammon].' It is not simply a question of two ways of using money but of the impossibility of any compromise between the service of God and of wealth – for mammon takes on the character of an idol. Yet it is not really a struggle between God and mammon. The conflict is situated in the human heart, in the psychological inability of giving oneself wholly to two masters, neither of whom can be served by half-measure. The service of the one or the other must be exclusive. One has to make a choice. The situation of the wealthy man is tragic: his wealth ties him to mammon. How difficult it is to free himself and place himself wholly in the service of God (see 18:24-25). And thus Luke's closing recommendation remains: 'And I tell you, make friends for yourselves by means of dishonest wealth ...' (v. 9). Wealth, or the acquiring of it, has a fatal propensity to dishonest conduct.

Dives and Lazarus (16:19-31)

In Luke's mind the two parables of his chapter 16 (the Astute Manager and Dives and Lazarus) have the same theme: the use of

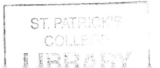

money. The Astute Manager, we have seen, was to teach the disciples (v.1) the proper use of money; Dives and Lazarus was to point out to the Pharisees the danger in which they stood because of their preoccupation with money (v. 14). Dives (the man is anonymous; he gets his traditional name form the Latin designation of him as *dives,* ('rich man') was a worldling who did not look beyond the good things of this life (v. 19). In sharp contrast stood the crippled (who 'lay' at his gate) beggar Lazarus – the name (Eliezer) means 'My God helps'. The dogs aggravated his outcast condition by rendering him ritually unclean (v. 21). He would have been glad to have – if they had been offered to him – the pieces of bread on which guests wiped their fingers and then dropped on the floor (vv. 20-21). The rich man might, according to Luke's understanding of v. 9 – 'And I tell you, make friends for yourselves by means of dishonest wealth, so that when it is gone they may welcome you into the eternal homes,' – have made of Lazarus a friend to welcome him into heaven. It is important to observe that nowhere is it suggested that Dives' wealth is ill-gotten nor that Lazarus is a victim of his oppression. The sin of Dives is that, cushioned by his lavish lifestyle, he was simply oblivious to the presence of a beggar at his gate. The contrast between the two in the next world is even more pronounced – but now they have exchanged roles (v. 22). 'To be with Abraham' echoes the description of death as 'being gathered to Abraham', that is, taken to join the patriarchs in Sheol. The rich man's burial, in keeping with his wealth, merely emphasised the futility of his life, for he went to the place of torment.

Jesus' story reflects the current vision of Sheol as it had been adapted in wake of belief in resurrection and retribution after death. It was imagined to have two compartments: in one the just quietly awaited resurrection; in the other the wicked were already being punished (vv. 23-24). Abraham did not disown Dives. As a Jew he was, according to the flesh, his son, but this was not enough to save him (vv. 25-26). We recall the warning of the Baptist: 'Do not begin to say to yourselves, "We have Abraham as our ancestor"; for I tell you, God is able from these stones to raise up children to Abraham' (3:8). The rich man understood that his present state was punishment, not a change of fortune only, and that Lazarus was being rewarded, not because there was any virtue in his poverty, but because God is vindicator of the poor. The abyss not only divides the respective compartments but marks a stark separation between the two classes of the dead. In all of this Jewish imagery, we are not given anything resembling a 'topography of hell'. Besides, the description purports to be of an intermediary stage.

This is one of the two-tiered parables and, true to form, the emphasis falls on the second part (vv. 27-31). But just as, in the first half, we are given no real description of 'hell', so here we can learn nothing of the psychology of the 'damned'. The reaction of Dives is described from an ordinary point of view: his present sorry state had at last opened his eyes and he was understandably desirous that his brothers should escape his fate (vv. 27-28). Abraham answered that the five, who evidently sported the same lifestyle as their unhappy brother, have 'Moses and the prophets,' that is, the Old Testament. A text of Isaiah meets exactly the situation: what God asks of his people is 'to share your bread with the hungry, and bring the homeless poor into your house; when you see the naked to cover him' (58:7). The man made one more bid (v. 30). Surely, if Lazarus were to come back from the dead the brothers would, at last, be moved to repent. The reply is that a miracle will not help those who have made no use of the means God had put at their disposal. Luke, and his readers, would have in mind the resurrection of Jesus and resistance to acceptance of it.

We must look to the broader context of Luke's attitude towards wealth. Why is it 'easier for a camel to go through the eye of a needle than for someone who is rich to enter the kingdom of God' (18:25)? The first 'woe' replies: because the rich 'have received their consolation' (6:24). The declaration of Abraham is explicit: 'Child, remember that during your lifetime you received your good things, and Lazarus in like manner evil things; but now he is comforted here, and you are in agony' (16:25). There is no doubt that Luke regarded the rich as unhappy and he invites us to pity them. The broad way along which they walk is not the path which leads to the Kingdom.

ALMS – *Eleémosyné*

The episode of the rich ruler (Lk 18:18-25) illustrates the extreme difficulty a rich person experiences when faced with the challenge

of the kingdom. Typically of the Lucan Jesus, the man was challenged: 'sell all that you have and distribute the money to the poor'
(v. 22). Inexorably, Luke maintains his position that the proper use
of wealth is to distribute it to the poor. Another dimension of the
episode is that it is a story of a sinner sought and found by Jesus. As
the conversion of a rich person it was an example to rich Christians
as to how they should comport themselves.

The term *eleémosyné* ('alms') – apart from Mt 6:2-3 – occurs in the
New Tesrtament only in Luke-Acts. It is a word coined by the
Septuagint translators. The LXX word for *hesed* – God's covenant
love – is *eleos;* its word for alms-giving echoes it: *eleémosyné* Almsgiving is a reflection of God's mercy towards his people, his mercy
which they are expected to imitate. 'Since there will never cease to
be some in need on the earth, I therefore command you, "open your
hand to the poor and needy neighbour in your land"' (Deut 15:1). In
his use of the term, Luke no doubt has in mind his mainly Gentile-
Christian community who (unlike their Jewish brothers and sisters)
had no tradition of almsgiving. The evidence is considerable that
almsgiving was not known among Graeco-Romans. Graeco-
Romans would not come to the aid of a non-citizen. They would
help a friend in need, but only to collect IOU's against future con-
tingencies.

When Luke uses the term 'alms' he has in mind first and foremost
those who are its recipients: destitute persons. His use of the word
expresses the duty of Christians to be compassionate to the poorest
of the poor. His poor – beggars and blind, lame, crippled left to their
own devises – are not members of the Christian community. He
took for granted that, among Christians, the poor would be cared
for (see Acts 2:42-47; 4:32-37). With his wider perspective, Luke
echoes the wider perspective of Jesus. After all, he had taken care to
record Jesus' definition of 'neighbour' (Lk 10:29-37).

The Lucan attitude to material possessions is not uncomplicated.
One may discern a two-fold stance: a moderate approach which
advocates a measured generosity in favour of the less fortunate,
and a radical approach which recommends the renunciation of all
wealth and possessions. One feels that Luke's own perspective is
uncomplicated: the only sensible thing to do with money is to give
it away in alms. But he is candid enough to acknowledge that his is

not the only view and he leaves place, in his gospel, for a moderate attitude (see 19:8).

SOCIAL ETHICS

Luke had in mind a group living as an independent community – or a close-knit group of communities – in a city of the Roman Empire. While it did not have members from the upper classes, it did not have destitute people either – beggars and so on. There were, nonetheless, serious tensions within the community. These were due, on the one hand, to economic differences: in addition to rich people there were others who, while not destitute, were poor – ordinary folk such as manual workers and the like. On the other hand, there were social tensions. Wealthy and respectable Christians looked down on the less well-off. This was a feature of their Hellenistic culture.

At the centre of the social message of Jesus in Luke are the instructions to the rich and respectable. They were offered a striking example in the person of Zacchaeus, the despised chief tax-collector. He renounced half his possessions: 'half of my possessions I will give to the poor' (19:8). The Lucan Jesus might have added, as after the parable of the Good Samaritan, 'Go and do likewise' (10:37). The duty of the rich is not to amass wealth for themselves but to be rich in God's sight – that is, to espouse the cause of the poor. Luke, as 'evangelist of the rich', does not mince words. He desires the salvation of the rich but he is convinced that it can be achieved only through radical renunciation of the wealth which he perceives to be a formidable obstacle: 'It is easier for a camel to go through the eye of a needle than for someone who is rich to enter the kingdom of God' (18:25).

When one takes Acts into account, one becomes acutely aware that Luke has a social goal in view: an equal distribution of property within the Christian community. In his picture of the first Christian community in Jerusalem he formulated his utopian vision of a group characterised by material and social equality.

> All who believed were together and had all things in common; they would sell their possesions and goods and distribute the proceeds to all, as any had need (Acts 2:44-45).

Now the whole group of those who believed were of one heart and soul, and no one claimed private ownership of any possessions, but everything they owned was held in common ... There was not a needy person among them, for as many as owned lands and houses sold them and brought the proceeds of what was sold. They laid it at the apostles' feet, and it was distributed to each as any had need (4:32-37).

Likely, Luke knew little about the actual situation in the earliest community, indeed he more than suggests that conditions may have been a good deal less rosy (e.g. Acts 6:1). He painted an ideal-ised picture: not as the first community was, but as he wanted his community to be. The real background to his idealised presentation was the deficiencies in his own community – at least what he regarded as deficiencies. The disturbing factor is that Luke's utopia catches, accurately, the vision of Jesus. For Jesus had about him a community of equals. He had explicitly rejected the social pattern of the world: 'It shall not be so among you...'.

WOMEN IN LUKE–ACTS

We have looked at the 'poor' mainly in terms of the economically poor. The term can carry a wider brief and include the marginal-ised. In the world of the day, women fell into that category. The gospel of Luke contains more material about women than the other gospels together. It insists that those who followed Jesus were both men and women: 8:1-3; 23:49; 24:9-11. While women are not corre-spondingly present in Acts, the believing community is regularly described as 'men and women' (Acts 5:14; 8:3,12; 9:2, 36-42). A group of men and women together had made up Jesus' followers. Later, men and women constituted the community of those who believed in Jesus.

In Lk 8:2-3 the women (Mary, Joanna, Susanna and 'many others'), healed by Jesus, served him and his disciples out of their resources. *Diakonein* means 'to serve' with the connotation of waiting on some-one. It was a traditional service of slaves and women. Jesus trans-formed the meaning of the term. 'Who is greater, the one who is at table or the one who serves? Is it not the one at the table? But I am among you as one who serves' (Lk 22:27). The Christian leader is to be 'like one who serves' (v. 26). *Ho diakonón* (one who serves) is now a honorific designation. The antithetical roles of servant and ruler are paradoxically coupled. To serve *(diakonein)*, a function proper to women, is applied to men who have a leadership role. It characterises the manner in which leadership ought to be exercised. It is obvious that, along the lines of this model, women should readily qualify for leadership. This did not happen. Instead we find that, in Acts, the serving terminology is applied exclusively to men. It means that, in practice, women who supported and served *(diakonein)* were excluded from leadership. Leadership positions were *de facto* reserved for men.

There is an intriguing factor. Luke gives in Acts 1:22-23 his criteria for being an apostle: 'So one of the men who had accompanied us during all the time that the Lord Jesus went in and out among us, beginning from the baptism of John until the day when he was taken up from us – one of these must become a witness with us to the resurrection.' Admittedly, the issue is the replacement of Judas in order to complete the number of the Twelve. Yet, the requirement does fit Luke's own understanding of 'apostle' in a wider sense. One must have been a disciple of Jesus from Galilee to Jerusalem. The women disciples ought to be obvious candidates (see Lk 8:2-3; 23:55- 56; 24:1-11, 22; Acts 1:14). They were excluded by an initial demand of maleness: 'one of the *men'*. There is no logic here. There is prejudice. Women appeared as the first witnesses of the Lord's resurrection – Lk 24:1-12. They spoke the truth, they fulfilled the demand of Deut 19:15 as to the acceptable number of witnesses: two, or better, three – there were several women (Lk 24:10). Yet, they were not believed. The reaction of the 'apostles' was spontaneous: 'These words seemed to them an idle tale, and they did not believe them' (v. 11). A whole group of women (v. 10) stood over against the whole group of men ('the eleven and all the rest,' v. 9). The detailed testimony ('all these things' v. 9) was refused, the women were rejected. The women had been confirmed as disciples: the message of the resurrection was addressed directly and completely to them. This was confirmation of their privileged place among the followers of Jesus. They were not acknowledged simply and solely because they were women.

When women in Acts are excluded from becoming apostles or from being leaders in other ways, this is a consequence of Luke's restricted and special concept of apostleship and acceptance of the public sphere as a man's world. So the public act of witness has to be carried out by men. This is nowhere justified in theological terms, and women are never explicitly adjured to keep silence or to be subordinate. What is demonstrated is a structure imposing silence. The narrative about the women on Easter morning shows this with considerable clarity (Lk 24:4-11). When the message fails to reach its destination, this is not due to the women, but because the men do not believe them. But this does not shake the relationship of power and the conclusion is therefore none the less a rejection of women's possibility to bear witness.[21]

Luke, in his two-volume work, conveys a double message. In his gospel he preserves strongly positive traditions about women and intimates an active role for them. He also reveals that male bias militated against a like role. The gospel evidence is that Jesus' own attitude to women was unconventionally positive. Paul had welcomed women as fellow ministers.[22] The change came about when the patriarchal household system was adopted as the model for the Christian community structure (see 1 Tim 2-3; Tit 2:1-10). Women were effectively marginalised. Despite, however, the situation evident throughout Acts, Luke has given a glimpse of an alternative route. His 'double message nurtures a dangerous remembrance.'[23]

CONCLUSION

Luke is evangelist of the rich and respected. This is to say, he wants to motivate them towards conversion in keeping with the social message of Jesus. If he is 'evangelist of the rich,' his message is challenge – not at all palatable to the wealthy. He is an exceptionally keen critic of the rich. But he does envisage their conv~.ion which, as he sees it, is possible only by way of radical renunciation – renunciation of half their possessions (or, ideally, of all of it), and by painful specific conduct – risky loans, cancellation of debts.

Luke had to face the problem of wealth in his own community. If there were no absolutely needy members, there were those relatively well-off. These were, by and large, the 'pharisees'; significantly, Luke charaterised Pharisees as 'lovers of money'. He was perceptively aware of two attitudes fostered by riches: a false sense of security and a lack of appreciation of and concern for the plight of the poor. Indeed, he was conscious that mammon might become one's god. He also had to inculcate the practice of almsgiving among people for whom almsgiving was not part of their culture. For that matter, Luke was convinced that relief of human need and suffering was the one, the only, positive contribution of money – 'you must give up all that you have'.

We do not know if his 'pharisees' responded. His remains a valid Christian option – it inspired Francis of Assissi. The New Testament gives ample evidence of broad pluralism; there are many ways of being Christian. But there are limits. Wealth should be a source of discomfort for one striving to live a Christian way. Indeed, any factor or attitude – power, wealth, prestige or whatever – that fails to value people first and above all else, is incompatible with the call of Jesus. 'Seek first the rule of God...' And the rule of God, the kingdom, is God as salvation for humankind. This is *the* message of Jesus.

Salvation for *humankind*. There is, insistently, the place of women in the church. It is a problem that cannot be wished away. Jesus came to bring good news to the poor, to welcome captives, to free the oppressed (Lk 4:18). It cannot be his will that his sisters remain second-class citizens in an institution that purports to be his *ekklésia*. The patriarchal model does not square with his teaching and practice. Only an assembly of brothers *and* sisters can truly constitute his church.

CHAPTER SIX

Friend of Sinners

This fellow welcomes sinners and eats with them (Lk 15:2)

The parables of Lk 15 which deal with the reprieve of sinners are Jesus' answer to the 'scandal' of the Pharisees: 'All the tax collectors and sinners were coming to listen to him. And the Pharisees and the scribes were grumbling and saying, "This fellow welcomes sinners and eats with them"' (15:1-2). The parables are a vindication of the good news for three reasons: because in them sinners are said to be sick people (only the sick need a doctor) and grateful people (only those burdened by debts can know the meaning of remission); because they reveal the nature of God as loving, merciful Parent; because they show 'sinners' as, in some way, closer to God than the 'righteous'. These parables reveal God's compassion for sinners, not as a timeless, general, truth but as realised in the ministry of Jesus. The lost sheep is dearer to this Shepherd, this Jesus, precisely because it is lost! The parables demonstrate that the words and actions of Jesus are inseparable. He is not a teacher of morals outlining principles of conduct. Instead, his attitude towards, and his daily life with, the poor are the model of our behaviour. He has fulfilled perfectly – as he no doubt inspired – the words of counsel given later to his followers: 'Little children, let us love, not in word or speech, but in truth and action' (1 Jn 3:18).

'I have come to call not the righteous but sinners' (Mt 9:13). The declaration is not only a scandal to the 'righteous' – it is hope for sinners. The sinners are thereby promised that God will intervene and that his doing so involves the remission of debts (as illustrated by the parables of the Two Debtors, the Unmerciful Servant and the Prodigal Son – Lk 7:41-43; Mt 18:23-35; Lk 15:11-32). Though Jesus promised only seldom 'forgiveness of sins' in as many words, the subjects of God's mercy and forgiveness were ever present in the rich picture language of his parables and sayings. The 'little ones' and the 'poor' are indeed privileged, but the privilege is not in themselves but solely in the heart of God – his *eudokia*, his generous benevolence. Jesus does not promise the poor and the humble a 'reward' for their way of life, but a share in the favour which God grants to what is little, weak and despised.

SINNERS

If we are truly to appreciate the scandal of the righteous at Jesus' befriending of sinners, we must understand who the sinners are. The term 'sinners' in the Old Testament refers to people who, in some fundamental way, stand outside the Law. A representative text is Psalm 10 where the 'wicked' *(reshaim)* are described as follows: 'In the pride of their countenance the wicked say, "God will not seek it out"; all their thoughts are, "There is no God"; They seize the poor ... the helpless fall by their might ... They think in their heart, "God has forgotten, he has hidden his face, he will never see it".' (Ps 10:4, 10-11). The LXX rendered *reshaim* by *hamartóloi* ('sinners') and Greek-speaking Jews used the term of the non-observant who had placed themselves outside the covenant. The 'sinners' of the gospels are these 'wicked' people regarded as living blatantly outside the Law. Jesus counted such within his fellowship. This was conduct that genuinely caused serious offence.[24]

Lost Sheep, Lost Coin (15:3-10).

Their Lucan setting (15:1-2) would fix the three parables of mercy credibly in the ministry of Jesus. The 'grumbling' of v. 2 – 'The Pharisees and the scribes were grumbling and saying, "This fellow welcomes sinners and eats with them"' – speaks so much. The Pharisees had set the Torah as the way of righteousness and had found in meticulous observance of it the achievement of righteousness. All who did not know the Law, or who did not keep it, were 'sinners', strangers to the way of righteousness. 'But this crowd, which does not know the law – they are accursed' (Jn 7:49). Jesus staunchly refused to categorise people; to him no one was outcast. The Pharisees could not bear that Jesus welcomed 'sinners' and sought them out. Worst of all, and there is a note of disgust, if not a note of horror: he 'eats with them' (see 5:30; 7:34). It was axiomatic that one could not have communion with 'sinners': contact with these outcasts rendered one ritually unclean. What right had this Jesus to flout so basic a requirement of the broader Torah?

Jesus countered their accusations by telling this parable (Lk 15:3) – three parables in fact: the Lost Sheep, the Lost Coin, the Lost Son. His defence was that he sought and welcomed the outcast because such is the Father's will. God is vindicator of the poor; the faithful Son was vindicator in turn. The outcasts, too, had caught the message. All their life they had been told that they stood beyond the pale. They were without hope, robbed of hope by the 'righteous'. Only an infinitely gracious God can forgive the devastation visited by the 'righteous' on 'sinners', in particular, by 'righteous' with pastoral responsibility. The plight of the 'outcasts' is well documented in the Pharisee and the Tax Collector (Lk 18:10-14). 'The tax-collector, standing far off, would not even look up to heaven, but was beating his breast and saying, "God, be merciful to me, a sinner!"' At the end of all, he could not really bring himself to accept that God was as the 'righteous' had painted him. At least, he dared to hope that he was not so. Now, such as he were given glowing hope. This man of God, unlike the righteous, did not shun them. No wonder that 'sinners' flocked to Jesus. And he, insultingly branded 'a friend of sinners', would have accepted the designation as the truest compliment. His meat was to do the will of him who had sent him (Jn 4:34). Nothing was dearer to the Father's heart than this loving concern for the outcast.[25]

In the parable of the Lost Sheep (15:4-7) Jesus tells of the shepherd who went in search of the sheep that was lost and of his joy when he found the stray. The solicitude of the man was such that he had left the ninety-nine in the desert, that is, in the scanty pasture of the Judaean hill-country, while he searched for the other. And his joy at finding the lost sheep was so great that he must tell his neighbours of it. The moral of the story is stated in emphatic terms: God will rejoice ('joy in heaven' is a circumlocution) that, together with the just, he can also welcome home the repentant sinner. Or, we might render the verse: 'Thus God, at the Last Judgment, will rejoice more over one sinner who has repented than over ninety-nine respectable persons who have not committed any gross sin.'

The shepherd is God: at a good deal of risk to the flock (sheep do not fend for themselves very well), God goes after a single lost sheep. God wants the sinner to come back, to be sure, but the emphasis falls entirely on God's search, not on the sinner's repentance. This is a parable of good news about God; it is not an illustration of the value of repentance. The good news about God is potentially a much more powerful message than a standard exhortation to give up wickedness and turn over a new leaf.[26]

That is why Jesus sought out sinners while the scribes and Pharisees, by caviling at his conduct, were questioning the divine goodness.

Peculiar to Luke, the Lost Coin (15:8-10) is parallel to the former parable. It is typical of this evangelist that he has brought a woman into the picture. The 'silver coins' (or, 'drachmas') represent a modest sum, but the loss of even one coin is of great concern to a woman in humble circumstances. She had to light a lamp because the small windowless house – the only opening being a low door – was in near darkness. The phrase 'in the presence of the angels of God' (v. 10) is a periphrastic rendering of the divine name: 'God will rejoice' (see v. 7; 12:8- 9). The two parables consider the conversion of a sinner from God's point of view: he rejoices that the lost should come back home, because they are his; he rejoices because he can forgive. God has sent his Son 'to seek out and to save the lost' (19:10), and Jesus' actual concern for sinners is a concrete proof that God does more than desire that sinners should repent.

REPENTANCE

Luke has a distinctive concern with repentance. In his gospel the words 'repent' and 'repentance' occur with notably more frequency than in Mark and Matthew. Compare Mk 2:17, 'I have come to call not the righteous but sinners', with Lk 5:32, 'I have come to call not the righteous but sinners to repentance.' Compare Mt 18:14, 'It is not the will of your Father in heaven that one of these little ones should be lost', with Lk 15:7, 'There will be more joy in heaven over one sinner who repents than one ninety-nine persons who need no repentance.' The fact is that 'repentance has a prominence in Luke that it does not have in Matthew and Mark ... Repentance has a prominence in Acts that it does not have in the rest of the New Testament, except the Book of Revelation.'[27]

The Lucan Jesus does set store by repentance. Even here, though, it is clear that Jesus in no way demanded repentance as a condition of his friendship. When one looks beyond Luke it is evident that Jesus cannot be characterised as a preacher of repentance. Tax-collectors are regularly associated with sinners as his friends. It would seem that they were despised not primarily because they were regarded as collaborators with the Roman regime, as is frequently asserted, but, simply, because they were suspected of making exorbitant demands and, therefore, of being exploiters. They were, effectively, ignoring God and his demands.

Jesus had tablefellowship with 'tax collectors and sinners'. He, in a manner that they could understand, assured them that God loved them. Doubtless, he hoped that they would change their ways, but he did not threaten. And he did not demand that they perform what the Law stipulated if they were to be reckoned as righteous. In spite of Luke's own emphasis on repentance, the distinctive, and scandalous, conduct of Jesus himself shines through his narrative. One thinks, for instance, of Zacchaeus in his sycamore tree. A preacher of repentance might have wagged the finger and read him the riot act – a spectacularly captive hearer. Instead, Jesus casually invited himself to dinner in his home. Zacchaeus must nearly have toppled from his perch in surprised delight. A sermon would have left him unaffected – he had been too often preached at. The novel approach changed his life (Lk 19:1-10).

Jesus was not 'soft' on sinners. He was, in fact, more radical than the reform-minded Baptist. He did not seek to enforce the commandments of the Jewish Law. What he did do, and his demand was gravely offensive, was to assert the significance of his own mission and authority. He did not oppose the Law but he did indicate that accepting him and following him were more important than observance. His friendship with sinners was, indeed, an emphatic claim. 'Through him, Jesus held, God was acting directly and immediately, bypassing the agreed, biblically sanctioned ordinances, reaching out to the lost sheep of the house of Israel with no more mediation than the words and deeds of one man – himself ... If the most important thing that people do was to accept him, the importance of other demands was reduced.'[28]

The Lost Boy (15:11-32)

The parables of the Lost Sheep and the Lost Coin carry the moral: God will rejoice over one sinner who repents. Both parables show the conversion of a sinner from God's point of view: he rejoices because he can forgive. The sheep and the coin represent the sinner who repents (a deed not easily achieved by sheep or coin!). Hence the Prodigal Son – better, the Lost Boy – with human characteristics. While the Lost Boy, in its present shape, is surely a composition of Luke, his inspiration was, authentically, Jesus. Only a conviction that he echoed the sentiment of a wholly merciful Saviour could account for the subversive, and wondrously comforting, tenor of this powerful story. Here the Lucan Jesus is – the concern with repentance aside – unquestionably *Jesus*.

The story of the father and his two sons is allegory; the characters are God, the sinner and the righteous. Jesus' purpose was not only to depict God's gracious forgiveness. It was to hold the mirror up to his opponents. It was to challenge them to see themselves in the elder son. Jesus' parable is a defence of his conduct, his concern for the 'little ones' whom the Pharisees had written off as outcasts. Defence, yes – yet profoundly challenging.

'There was a man who had two sons.' The younger of the brothers asked his father for the share of the family property that would fall to him – one third of the estate. He, evidently, turned his share into cash and set off. His money was quickly squandered in dissolute living and his erstwhile friends left him in the lurch. He had struck rock-bottom: a Jew herding pigs. He even envied the pigs who had something to eat. He cannot share *their* meal; he cannot have table-fellowship with pigs! In his degradation he 'came to himself'. And his thought was of his father. He will return, confess his folly, acknowledge his unworthiness. Maybe he will be received back as a 'hired hand'.

'He got up and went.' This is what the father had hoped for, had longed for. Ever on the look-out, he spied the hapless homecomer and hastened to welcome him. Not a word of reproof. Stirred only by loving compassion, he embraced and kissed the lost one. *All* is forgiven. The son's little speech was no longer confession (as his rehearsed speech was intended to be); it was spontaneous response to forgiveness. There were no strings to this forgiveness. Best robe, signet ring, shoes: the youth was reinstated. He is son as though he had never left, had never gone astray. Nor is this the end. It was a moment to be savoured, a time for joymaking. Such is God's forgiveness, Jesus says. God casts our sins behind his back; he buries them in the deeps of the sea (see Is 38:17; Mic 7:18-19).

Jesus' Jewish hearers would have grasped the pathos of the young man's plight. What they would have found disconcerting was the incredible conduct of the father. To receive back, without a word of reproof and without any condition at all, one who had shown himself so weak and untrustworthy, was incredibly foolish. They would have identified, readily, with the hardnosed other son. Yet, the fact that the story itself manifestly extolled the conduct of the father would have given pause. What is it all about? It is too much for humankind, as the second part of the parable brings out.

The elder son is, recognisably, the 'scribe and pharisee'. He was quite upset when he learned that the unexpected feast was to celebrate his erring brother's return. Again the father 'goes out' – his love reaches to all. But the elder son was indignant at the injustice of the situation. He did not say 'Father' as the other had; he spoke of 'working like a slave' and of 'obeying your command'. The younger son had been prepared to settle for servanthood. The other had the mentality of a 'hired hand', the mind of a slave. That is why he could not understand the father's love, why he was shocked by that display of love. He had disowned his brother who is 'this son of yours'. He was, however, gently reminded that the returned one was 'this brother of yours'. And he was assured: 'You are always with me, and all that is mine is yours.' He was still the heir. His brother's return offered no threat.

Jesus would suggest that the weakness of the younger son is *vulnerability*. He was vulnerable both to his fair-weather friends and to the love of his father. The rectitude of the elder son was effective armour against the plea of vulnerability and the foolishness of love. He had never really known his father and now he rejected his brother who had besmirched the family name. Had he not a point? To receive back, without sanction, one who had already proved fickle, was rash in the extreme. It was crass favouritism – this cossetting of a profligate and neglect of one who had always served and obeyed! The story ends, not with an explanation of such conduct but with an invitation: the elder son is invited to acknowledge his brother and enter into the joy of homecoming. Only so will he know his father as *father*.

The ending of the parable (vv. 31-32) is an example of the literary feature of unresolved conflict. Its purpose is to involve the readers/hearers. They are made to wonder how they would have acted had they found themselves in the situation of the elder son. The story is not rounded off precisely because the readers are invited to write its ending.

This story was Jesus' answer to the 'grumblers' – the begrudgers. He told them that God is supremely concerned with those whom they had branded and spurned as outcasts. He told them that he shared the concern of his Father: 'I have come to call not the righteous but sinners' (Mk 2:17). In Luke's setting the story is even more provocative. Luke's 'sinners' and 'pharisees' are *Christians*. He was exercised by the intolerance of 'righteous' Christians. For them, God's mercy to sinners was scandal: it is not fair. And if, indeed, God is one to be served, if he is one who has set firm rules that must be kept, then it is unfair that one should be saved without obeying the rules and without rendering service. That God should be more concerned with the wayward ones than with his faithful servants is intolerable. Many Christians would empathise with the elder son. Any who do so, whether they are aware of it or not, share his image of God. It is not Jesus' understanding of the Father.

The truth is that those for whom God is loving Parent will not be resentful, because they understand the crazy logic of love. They will enter gladly into the rejoicing. They, as brothers and sisters, will share the Father's yearning for the homecoming of the lost ones. They know that this Father's love is inexhaustible, know that they will not be loved less because the Father's love embraces others. They will love the Father for his generosity. Every gesture of forgiveness will remind them of the forgiveness they had received, of the love lavished upon them. They will understand that Jesus had sought out sinners precisely because he had known the Father's love. They will seek to enter more deeply into that love, they will want to rejoice at that generosity.

Yet, at the end of all, did not the elder son have a point? Was the father not being unwise, was he not taking a risk? To receive back, without condition, one who had already proved fickle – was that not to encourage him to take advantage of such generosity? Of course there was risk; but the father did not hesitate. His hope was that the son would recognise love and would respond with generosity. He will use no other means than love. What is quite clear is that if the son were to go off again, and again come home, he would meet with the self-same mercy. Could Jesus seriously have urged that our forgiveness of one another be without limit (Mt 18:21-35) if he did not know that the Father's forgiveness knows no bounds?

On many counts this is a disturbing story for us Christians of today. Luke took it out of the ministry of Jesus and addressed it directly to the 'pharisees' in his own Christian community. And, surely, we must look to ourselves, to our possible resentment of God's graciousness to sinners. We can find comfort in the warm treatment of the younger son. Always, there is the father. He is the real challenge. Our gracious and forgiving God holds the stage. This story persuasively shows God's loving concern for humankind and, in particular, his favouritism towards the outcast. It sets a question-mark against the theology of forgiveness reflected in much of our penitential practice. God's forgiveness seems too good to be true. Above all, there is the uncomfortable message that one really comes to understand this Father only by acknowledging the brother and sister as brother and sister – a lesson learned by the author of 1 John: 'Those who do not love a brother or sister whom they have seen cannot love God whom they have not seen' (4:20).

Zacchaeus (19:1-10)

In this episode Jesus showed himself a friend of 'tax collectors and sinners' and again his solicitude met with criticism (see 15:1-2). Zacchaeus held a high position at an important customs post and had turned it to good account. Curious to see a man with such a reputation as Jesus had won, Zacchaeus forgot his dignity (19:3-4). It was Jesus who spotted Zacchaeus. He 'must' come to the house of the tax collector, he who had come to seek out 'the lost' (v. 10). The joy of Zacchaeus was matched by the murmuring of those who did not understand the goodness of God (vv. 6-7; see 5:30; 15:2). Touched by the gracious approach of Jesus (v. 8), the tax collector was a changed man – he was more generous than the righteous ruler (18:23). The present tense – 'I am giving half of my possessions to the poor' – describes not a present habit but a present resolve: henceforth he will give half of his goods in alms. Moreover, he will make fourfold amends (the requirement of Roman law in *furtum manifestum*) if he can ascertain that he had defrauded anybody.[29] Luke's concern with the proper use of wealth (to give it away in alms!) is evident. Jesus declared to Zacchaeus in effect: 'Today salvation has come to this house' (v. 9). But in Luke's narrative this verdict is strictly linked to the declaration of the rich tax collector in v.8. Zacchaeus is saved but his fortune is gone back to the poor. Inexorably, Luke maintains his position that the proper use of wealth is to distribute it to the poor.

Jesus turned to the grumblers – 'All who saw it began to grumble and said, "He has gone to be the guest of one who is a sinner".' His rejoinder was positive and emphatic: 'Today salvation has come to this house, because he too is a son of Abraham' (v. 9). Zacchaeus was a son of Abraham and had as much right to the mercy of God as any other Israelite (see 13:16); the visit of Jesus had brought salvation to the man and his family. V. 10 – 'For the Son of Man came to seek out and save the lost' – is very likely an independent saying which echoes the theme of the parables of chapter 13 and indeed of the whole gospel. The Zacchaeus episode is a striking illustration of it.

Response to Forgiveness (7:36-50)

Virtually everything that the early church remembered about John the Baptist had to do with repentance in view of imminent judgment. A summary statement has Jesus preaching repentance in view of the nearness of the kingdom: 'The time is fulfilled, and the kingdom of God has come near; repent and believe in the good news' (Mk 1:15). While there is a summons to repent, it is surely not the whole message. Jesus himself was not primarily a preacher of repentance; he proclaimed the imminent coming of the kingdom as *salvation*. The parables of God seeking the lost (Lk 15:3-6, 8-9), once Luke's conclusions (15:7, 10) are removed, can be seen as focused not on repentance but on God's initiative and action. The one distinctive note that we can certainly discern in Jesus' teaching on the kingdom is that it would involve 'sinners' – the wicked. Jesus was accused of associating with, and offering the kingdom, to those who by the normal standards of Judaism were sinners.[30]

If there is the central reality of divine forgiveness, there is also the factor of human response to forgiveness. This is presented by Luke in an unforgettable manner. Nowhere more clearly than in Lk 7:36-50, the story of 'a woman in the city who was a sinner' (v. 37) do we see Jesus as Luke saw him. The context, too, is admirable: here indeed is the 'friend of sinners' (v. 34). The story has links with other anointing stories: Mk 14:3-9; Jn 12:1 – the story had assumed various forms in the stage of oral tradition. Here the Pharisee (Simon, v. 40), though he had invited Jesus to dine with him, had been coldly formal in the reception of his guest (vv. 44-46). Though 'sinner' is of wider connotation, the impression is that this woman was a prostitute and was well known as such (v. 30). Luke has court-eously refrained from naming her and she must remain anony-mous. She was a woman who had previously encountered Jesus and had received his forgiveness. She had come to thank him. She made a brave and extravagant gesture. She, a woman and a sinner to boot, dared to crash this 'stag party'. She kissed and anointed the feet of a reclining Jesus, to the evident scandal of his Pharisee host. Jesus, on the other hand, accepted her presence and ministry with gentle courtesy. And his verdict was clear and to the point: 'Her great love proves that her sins have been forgiven' (v. 47). Simon's reasoning was: if Jesus were so unaware of the character of the woman that he had now incurred the ritual uncleanness of contact with a sinner, then he could not be the prophet whom many believed him to be.

The money-lender of Jesus' parable (vv. 41-43), who remits debts simply because his debtors were unable to pay, is hardly typical of his calling. It is manifest that close behind him stands a God who is ready to forgive any debts. Such is God, Jesus says, infinitely good and merciful. In the parable – 'now which of them will love him more?' (7:42) – 'love' means 'thankful love', 'gratitude'; so the ques-tion of Jesus would run: 'Which of them would be the more grate-ful?' While Simon had omitted those gestures of esteem and affec-tion with which an honoured guest was received, the woman has so prodigally supplied them (vv. 44-47). Simon is the target of the parable and is bluntly told: This woman, despite her sinful past, is

nearer to God than you, for she has, what you lack, love and gratitude.

MARY MAGDALENE

This is by way of appendix. It is, I believe, highly important. The
woman of Lk 7:36-50 is anonymous. Unhappily, in Christian tradition, she has been identified as Mary Magdalene. In this, tradition
has been cruel to Mary. Indeed, she could well qualify as the most
sinned against victim of sexist prejudice. Her characterisation as a
reformed prostitute has gone almost unchallenged. The fact is:
there is not a single shred of evidence to sustain that portrait of her.
She has had the ill fortune to emerge for the first time in Luke's
gospel immediately after his story of 'the sinner' (7:36-50). Whether
or not that sinner was a prostitute (not wholly clear) has nothing to
do with the subsequent reference to 'Mary, called Magdalene, from
whom seven demons had gone out' (8:2). Traditionally, the 'seven
demons' have been identified as demons of sexual immorality and
Mary has been identified with the anonymous woman of chapter 7
(who was taken to be a prostitute). The only logic here is the sick
logic of misogyny. From parallel texts (see Mk 5:8; Lk 11:26) it is
clear that possession by 'seven demons' means that Mary was a
mentally ill woman, healed by Jesus. To class her as 'sinner' is
calumny.

One is not suggesting that a one-time sinner might not become a
follower of Jesus and a saint. But there is no justification for classify-
ing Mary Magdalene as a reformed prostitute. Perhaps the whole of
feminine unhappiness with the church is just there. The thoroughly
positive presentation of Mary Magdalene in the Synoptic – and more
so in the Johannine – traditions has been adroitly manipulated. The
threatening Mary has been cut down to size: she is the proverbial
prostitute with the heart of gold. Personally, I take every opportunity
to 'rehabilitate' Mary Magdalene. I do so, not only from a sense of
justice but as a scripture scholar. Mary of Magdala is the most
prominent woman in our gospel tradition

CONCLUSION

Jesus was not primarily a preacher of repentance; he proclaimed the
imminent coming of the kingdom as *salvation*. The parables of God
seeking the lost (Lk 15:3-6, 8-9), once Luke's conclusions (15:7,10)

are removed, can be seen as focused not on repentance but on God's initiative and action. The one distinctive note that we can be certain marked Jesus' teaching about the kingdom is that it would include the 'sinners'. There should be no confusion about the basic meaning of the term 'sinners' in the gospels. It comes from the Hebrew *reshaim* – the wicked. Jesus saw his mission as being in a special manner to the 'lost' and the 'sinners'. He was also concerned with the poor, the meek and the downtrodden. If there was conflict, it was about the status of the *wicked*: 'This fellow welcomes sinners and even eats with them!'

We have, unhappily, tended to imagine divine forgiveness in terms of a human model. Indeed, consistent with our, too often, flawed image of God, we assume that such forgiveness is reluctant: an offended deity is ready to forgive, provided he gets his pound of flesh. It is a sad travesty of God's forgiveness, yet one that is prevalent. Our Parent forgives, eagerly, wholly, if we give him the chance. 'I will get up and go to my Father': a turning to him is all he asks. He – and he alone – can and will do the rest. To seek God's forgiveness is a homecoming; to be forgiven is to be welcomed home. It is a joyous moment, to be savoured and celebrated.

The stories of the woman sinner and of Zacchaeus show that Jesus was not in the business of saving 'souls'; he was concerned with *people*. In relation to women, given the culture of his day, he was unconventional. His band of disciples was a mixed group of men and women. Jesus was friend of sinners – he brought hope into their lives. As 'image of the invisible God' he imaged the *Deus humanissimus* – the God bent on the salvation of humankind.

CHAPTER SEVEN

Prayer

Lord, teach us to pray (Lk 11:1)

'Descended from David according to the flesh' (Rom 1:3), Jesus was a son of Israel. As a committed Israelite he was, by definition, a man of prayer. Aside from Luke, who had a special interest in prayer, the evangelists do not elaborate on Jesus' prayer-life. That is not surprising. Simply, they, like him, took prayer for granted. We, Christians of another culture and of the twentieth – soon to be twenty-first – century, cannot be so casual. We demand reasons for everything and we do ask why we ought to pray in the first place. The realisation that Jesus was a man of prayer may give us food for thought.

There is no doubt at all that Jesus did pray. For that matter, even if the gospels had no word of his prayer, we could still be certain that he did pray, for prayer was second nature to any believing Jew. We do not need to speculate. Mark, with attractive candour, tells us that Jesus' addiction to prayer was something of a trial to his disciples. The evangelist has given a sample day in the early Galilean ministry, at Capernaum (Mk 1:21-34), a day of enthusiastic reception and of great promise. His disciples, caught up in the excitement, were chagrined when Jesus went missing (v. 37) – 'In the morning, while it was still very dark, he got up and went out to a deserted place, and there he prayed' (1:35). Typically, Mark has said much in few words. Jesus had slept (he 'got up'), had snatched a few hours of sleep. For his mission he needed deeper refreshment, a more potent source of energy, and he found it in prayer to his Abba. His Father was the Sustainer of all. As one 'like us in every respect' (Heb 2:17), Jesus was wholly dependent on this God. He turned, spontaneously, to an Abba who would support him, who would back him in his endeavours. True, he was sent, one who had to plough his own furrow. But he was not alone because the Father was with him. The prayer of Jesus, his whole prayerful trust in his Abba, is an essential ingredient of any meaningful christology.

Prayer of Jesus

Prayer of and by Jesus, by example, not by contrived design, is meant to alert the disciple to his or her dependence on God. If the Son found a need and a joy in converse with his Father, he could expect that the other children of God, his sisters and brothers, would, too, experience that need and that happiness. The comforting fact is that Jesus, as our high priest, has not ended his prayer. Returned to the Father, he has no need, any more, to pray for himself. Henceforth, he is the high priest who prays *for us,* who makes intercession for us, without respite (see Heb 7:25).

It ought not surprise us that the prayer of Jesus should figure in the gospel of Luke. The third evangelist, with his notable interest in prayer, could not have overlooked the prayer of the Lord. It is he who tells us that Jesus prayed at the baptism: 'Now when all the people were baptised, and when Jesus had been baptised and was praying, the heaven was opened, and the Holy Spirit descended upon him in bodily form like a dove. And a voice came from heaven, "You are my Son, the Beloved; with you I am well pleased"' (Lk 3:21-22). Luke, indeed, gives the impression that it was as response to the prayer of Jesus that the Holy Spirit came upon him. And not impression only; it is Luke's intent that we should see it so. Later (1:13), we learn that the heavenly Father gives the Holy Spirit to those who ask. Jesus' prayer was a plea to the Father – not unlike the prayer of Job, though here apart from the context of distress – that God would manifest himself, would declare their relationship.

A phrase of Luke is revealing when we compare parallel gospel passages. Mark and Matthew agree that Jesus, on coming to 'his hometown' (which Luke names as Nazareth) on a sabbath, began to teach (Mk 6:1-2; Mt 13:54). Luke made a further point: 'Jesus went to the synagogue on the sabbath day, as was his custom' (Lk 4:16) – Jesus is characterised as a 'regular church-goer'. Luke does not have it all his own way. One might even say that, because of Luke's avowed interest in prayer, reference to the prayer of Jesus by the other evangelists has added weight. At least it assures us that Luke had latched on to a firm datum of the tradition.

According to the three synoptists Jesus prayed in Gethsemane, he prayed after the multiplication of loaves, he prayed in Capernaum after he had healed many. Luke speaks of the prayer of Jesus in eight further circumstances. He prayed at the baptism (Lk 3:21), he slipped away to a lonely place to pray (5:16), and, before selecting the Twelve, he spent the whole night in prayer (6:12). He prayed before Peter's confession of him as Messiah (9:18); later he would tell Peter that he had prayed especially for him (22:32). He prayed at the transfiguration (9:28-29) and it was sight of him at prayer that moved his disciples to ask him to be taught how to pray (11:1). He prayed on the cross for all who had engineered his death (22:34). The surrender of his life to the Father was a prayer (23:46).

Jesus had often recommended prayer to his disciples: persevering prayer like that of the importunate friend (11:5-13) or of the widow faced with an unjust judge (18:1-8). They must pray to receive the Holy Spirit (11:13). In short, they ought to pray at all times (21:36). But, their prayer should be real prayer, like that of the tax collector (18:13).

It Will Be Given (11:9-13)

'So I say to you, ask and it will be given you; search and you will find; knock, and the door will be opened for you' (11:9). Ask – search – knock ... can we square this exhortation with the assurance that 'your Father knows what you need before you ask him' (Mt 6:8)? Readily. God does not need us; he does not need our prayer. We need God; we need to acknowledge our dependence on God. 'Dependence' can carry unsavoury overtones; in human matters it is, too often, a degrading term. In a context of creature and Creator, dependence can have another meaning. The human creature is, in God's creation, the closest creature to God. As creature one depends wholly on one's Creator. There is nothing demeaning in this dependence. We may, in human conduct, find a key to an understanding of it. There is the dependence of an infant on a mother. When this is instinct with love, as it is meant to be, it is a thing of beauty. It is heartening to see how, for instance, in bus or train or plane, sight of a young mother absorbed in the gurgling tot in her arms wins spontaneous nods and smiles. That baby is *revelling* in dependence. The mother is certainly not domineering. The relationship is inescapable. The infant is wholly dependent. Only in acceptance of dependence can the child hope to grow to maturity of womanhood or manhood.

It is the same with humankind in relation to God. We are, whether we will or not, God's creatures, dependent on God. And only in union with God can we become wholly human. We must acknowledge our dependence; we must seek and knock. The need is ours, not his. And the answer will be his. The analogy of mother and child may serve us again. A loving mother knows what is good for her child. The child may ask, may demand; but she will grant only what is helpful. A firm 'No' is often the loving answer. A loving Parent will give, will open the way – but only when it is best. We should not forget that 'No' is quite as much an answer as 'Yes' – even to prayer! Indeed, this is a fact that Jesus experienced. At Gethsemane he prayed: 'Father, if you are willing, remove this cup from me; yet, not my will but yours be done' (Lk 22:42). The cup was not removed; he tasted its bitterness to the dregs. The author of Hebrews understood. He declared: 'He was heard because of his reverent submission' (Heb 5:7). Jesus had heard a compassionate but firm 'No.'

The human analogy does, of course, break down. A parent will not give a live snake or a venemous scorpion to a child who asks for bread (Lk 11:11-12). The heavenly Parent's giving, on the contrary, may, often enough, appear hurtful. At first, his fish and egg may seem to be serpent and scorpion. We may well ask: 'Why did God do this to me?' Where there is littleness and faith it will, in time, become clear that his gift is always goodness. Typically, Luke has transformed the original text. The 'good gifts' of the Father's bounty (Mt 7:11) have become for him the gift *par excellence,* source of all goodness: 'how much more will the heavenly Father give the Holy Spirit to those who ask him!' (Lk 11:13). The Holy Spirit, God's supreme gift, is answer to our deepest prayer.

The Lord's Prayer (11:1-4)

Luke has created a credible setting for the Lord's Prayer (11:1-3). It is not only that the disciples were, understandably, taken by the mien of Jesus in prayer to the Father (v. 1). They had come to regard themselves as a group apart, a group, in their eyes, as distinctive as the followers of the Baptist. (This might be seen as a further indication that Jesus had been originally a disciple of the Baptist. He had emerged as a prophet in his own right.) It was time for them to have their very own prayer: 'Lord, teach us to pray, as John taught his disciples' (v. 1). And that prayer will remain, for all time, the characteristic prayer of the disciples of Jesus. Matthew (6:9-13) and Luke have given two versions of the prayer. The first, obvious, difference is that Matthew's form is longer. More importantly, Matthew has presented the original, strongly eschatological flavour of it, while Luke has adapted it to the modest pattern of day-to-day Christian living.

On the other hand, Luke's simpler 'Father' (in place of the solemn 'our Father in heaven' of Matthew) is the intimate *Abba* of Jesus' own address. He invites his disciples to come to the Parent in a like uninhibited manner. 'Give us each day our daily bread' (v. 3) is a child-like request for the normal needs of life. Christians, even when they do look to a goal beyond earthly confines, must yet steadfastly live out their lives in the only world they know. They have need of One who will care for them. The God who arrays the lilies of the field and the birds will not neglect his human children (Mt 6:25-33; 12:22- 31). The disturbing truth is that daily bread is not for all and that little ones do go in need. Is this because we have not taken the whole message to heart: 'But strive first for the kingdom of God and his righteousness, and all these things will be given to you as well' (Mt 6:33)? Chesterton may have had the right of it when he observed that Christianity had not failed – because it had not been tried. More to the point, prayer, like the Christian view of things in general, needs to accept realistically the brokenness of our world. Luke has softened the Semitic starkness of the call to forgiveness (see Mt 6:12). It remains, for him, an inescapable obligation: 'forgive ... for we ourselves forgive' (Lk 11:4). Do we – can we – sincerely pray this prayer? An honest answer will tell us something of the quality of our Christianity.

Matthew has the Lord's Prayer in the setting of a warning against ostentation in performing the traditional good works of almsgiving, prayer and fasting (6:1-18). He has, on the admonition to quiet, hidden prayer (6:5-6), built a little catechesis on prayer: how not to pray (vv. 7-8), the model prayer (vv. 9-13) and has developed the petition on forgiveness (vv. 14- 15). He does not need to exhort his

Jewish-Christian readers to pray. He feels only that they may have a wrong slant on prayer. Luke, also, has his catechesis, again in relation to the Lord's Prayer (Lk 11:3-13). He has Gentile Christians in view. They had not the native feeling for prayer of their Jewish brothers and sisters. They need to be made aware of the generosity of their Parent and assured that their prayer will be heard. They must be encouraged to persevere in prayer.

PRAYER PARABLES

The Friend at Midnight (11:5-8)

Luke finds Jesus' teaching on prayer in his parables: perseverance in prayer (11:5-13; 18:1-8) and humility in praying (18:9-14). The parable of the Friend at Midnight (11:5-8) is, in its Lucan setting, addressed to the disciples who had asked to be taught how to pray (11:1). Originally, in the setting of Jesus' ministry, the parable would have made its point through the conduct of the one who had been importuned. The phrase 'suppose one of you' means 'Can you imagine that you would act so?' and invites an indignant, 'Of course not!' In that case, Jesus told his hearers, you cannot imagine that God will reject the plea of one who calls upon him. With the suggestion that God might in any sense be like this boor ('Do not bother me') we are in the line of the daring familiarity of Old Testament prayer – as exemplified by Moses, Jeremiah and Job, and throughout the Psalter.

In Luke's context the focus is on the one who pleads. He had come, in need, to a friend. The situation was urgent. A friend of his had called on him, unexpectedly, and he must be given hospitality. The other, though roused from sleep at midnight, ought to have appreciated the gravity of the situation. In the drift of the story he has shown himself insensitive to the normal eastern feeling for the claim of hospitality. Very well – if the pleader will keep up his pestering he will be given what he wants, if only to be rid of him! When we recall that this is teaching on prayer to God we can savour, also, in this setting, the daring of it. Even when the emphasis has switched to perseverance, the implication is still that God is one to be worn down. Jeremiah and Job would feel at home with the parable. And the Christian should take heart from the fact that the Lord could present such a visage of the Father – if only to insist he is wholly other.

The Unjust Judge (18:1-8)

Luke makes clear his understanding of the parable of the Unjust Judge: the disciples should pray at all times and persevere in it (see 1 Thes 5:17). And he has in mind the coming of the kingdom; it will come in response to the prayer of God's elect for vindication. In reality, like the Friend at Midnight (Lk 1:5-8), the parable originally had a different emphasis. The judge in 18:6 is described as unjust. It is implied that the widow has right on her side, but the judge was not interested in the rights of a penniless plaintiff. If he is to give a decision in favour of anybody it has to be made worth his while to do so.

Jesus would have invited his readers to contemplate, if they would, a God cast in the mould of the unjust judge. Could they really imagine that he was remotely like that? It is the widow who holds Luke's attention – with the bonus that he has now balanced his male-role parable (11:5-8) with this female-role parable. The widow, aware that she cannot pay the bribe expected by this venal judge, has no recourse but to pester. If she makes enough of a nuisance of herself he will grant her request merely for the sake of peace and quiet. What a bold picture of prayer to God this is!

The parable is rounded off by an *a fortiori* argument. If this cynical judge will, in the end, yield to the importunity of the persistent widow, surely it is to be expected that God, who is not a judge at all but a loving parent, will yield to the importunity of his children! No, God will not delay. As always, the problem is not with the constant God; it is with the inconstant creature: 'When the Son of Man comes will he find faith on earth?' (18:8). Is there the faith that will support confident and persevering prayer? Each Christian must answer for herself and himself.

The Pharisee and the Tax Collector (18:9-14)

The parable of the Pharisee and the Tax Collector does fit neatly into the ministry of Jesus. Both characters are drawn from life: the righteous one and the outcast. And the parable was spoken as warning to the righteous: 'He told this parable to some who trusted in themselves that they were righteous and regarded others with contempt'(18:9).

So often the Pharisee of this parable has been called a hypocrite. It is an error which clouds the pathos of the parable and blunts its impact. The sad fact is that the man is sincere and his claims are true. He is scrupulously honest, a faithful family man, a meticulous observer of the Law (as the tax collector, by definition, is not). The Law enjoined only one fast a year (on the Day of Atonement) but he, a pious Pharisee, fasted each Monday and Thursday. And, far beyond the demands of the Law, he paid tithe on all his possessions. He was sincerely convinced that he stood right with God. After all, he had done what he ought to have done, and more. He can truly thank God that he is not as other people. The snag is that his 'prayer' is not prayer at all. That is why it was not heard.

It is this sort of person and this attitude Paul has in mind in Galatians and Romans. He had seen with clarity (he, too, had been a convinced Pharisee, Phil 3:5-6) that one for whom the heart of religion is observance may feel that one can earn salvation. What one must do and must avoid are clear. If one is faithful, then a just man cannot but justify one. Such an attitude blunts the perception that salvation is grace. That is why the Pharisee could not recognise God's gracious gift in Jesus. And it is because the 'sinner' had no illusion about his own state that he could instinctively recognise the gift for what it was. There is nothing mysterious in the fact that Jesus was a 'friend of tax collectors and sinners' nor that this was scandal to the 'righteous'. It is important to realise that, in the gospels, the Pharisees, for historical and polemical reasons, get a bad press. They are cast as legalistic rigorists with little respect for people, with contempt for ordinary folk. This is less than fair. Paul was proud of his Pharisaic past (Phil 3:5). But he had come to recognise the danger that committed observance might be perceived as a way of *earning* salvation.

There is a wry point to the story of the good lady who, after a Sunday morning homily on our parable, was heard to remark: 'Thank heaven, I am not like that Pharisee!' For, 'pharisaism' is not only a late Jewish phenomenon. It is endemic in the Christian church and has proved a hardy growth. The self-righteous Christian is not a rarity. Regular church-going and certain pious practices may seem to set one apart and guarantee salvation. Always, of course, it is a case of 'these you ought to have practised, without neglecting the others' – but the 'weightier matters' of justice, mercy and faith are what religion is about (Mt 23:23-24).

CONCLUSION

Prayer is a Christian need. We are children of God and should turn, with childlike directness, to our Parent. In this world we are sisters and brothers of the Brother who walked his way to Calvary. The Christain way, lived by Jesus, so firmly proposed by him and by his earliest disciples, is a way that challenges us. It is a way we dare not walk alone. But we are not alone, for he is with us. We meet him in our prayer and keep step with him on the way. He has taught us to pray to the Father, and we have learned to pray to him.

Conviction of the companionship of God was the secret of Jesus' own prayer life. What moved him to rise a long while before dawn to go out and pray in a lonely place so that he was long absent from his disciples (see Mk 1:35)? Or what made him go 'out to the mountain to pray, and to spend the night in prayer to God' (Lk 6:12)? In short, what was it that moved him to mark his prayer with the new, intimate mode of address: Abba? It was his abiding sense of communion with the Father, his knowing he was never alone.

That which Jesus felt with his Father was the same companionship his disciples, and all Christians, came to feel with him. This is movingly portrayed in the Emmaus narrative wherein Cleopas and his companion had the comfort of his fellowship when 'Jesus himself came near and went with them' – when he, unknown to them, walked along beside them and then 'went in to stay with them' at eventime (Lk 24:13-35). There, as they broke bread together, they came to recognise their Lord, the one whom they had been given as their Friend. They had opened their door to him, and he came in to sup with them and they with him (see Rev 3:20). He vanished from their sight, but their eyes had been opened – to know he was with them always, and that this itself would be their prayer.

The basis, the source of prayer, is faith – and the faith is faith in Jesus. It is the believing that is not afraid to ask, because this he wants: 'Ask, and it will be given you; search and you will find; knock, and the door will be opened for you' (Lk 11:9), for who would give his child a snake if he asked for food, and will not the heavenly Father even more give to his children the good things of their asking (see 11:11-13). After all, he does know what we need before we ask him (see Mt 6:8).

We recall again the road to Emmaus: Jesus drew near and went with his disciples. He continued with them and then 'walked ahead as if he were going on', until they stopped him and asked him, 'Stay with us, because it is almost evening and the day is now nearly over' (Lk 24:28-29). They asked, and so he answered: he went in to stay with them, he became known to them in the breaking of bread, and he opened their eyes. 'Stay with us': this, at heart, is the recurrent prayer of the Bible, the longing of the psalmist who wanted to dwell in the Lord's house all the days of his life. 'Stay with us': it is the prayer ever answered by our believing, 'I am with you always ...'

CHAPTER EIGHT

Death and Vindication

Was it not necessary that the Messiah should suffer these things and then enter into his glory? (Lk 24:26)

The four evangelists tell essentially the same story, but do so each in a distinctive manner. The fourth gospel obviously stands apart from the others. But, even among the Synoptics, differences are marked. This is so even in the area where all the evangelists meet most fully, in the passion narratives. One needs but compare Mark and Luke.

Mark's gospel is a *theologia crucis* – a theology of the cross. Understandably, this concern comes to a head in his passion narrative. It is evident in the Gethsemane episode (Mk 14:32-44) – 'he began to be distressed and agitated' (v. 33): Jesus is shattered. He died with an anguished shout: 'My God, my God, why have you forsaken me?' (15:34). Mark has Jesus die in total isolation, without any relieving feature at all. It is only after death that Jesus is clearly recognised and acknowledged by any human in the awed confession of the centurion: 'Truly, this man was God's Son!' (15:39). Mark is making a theological point: salvation is never of oneself, not even for Jesus. That awful and awesome journey to the cross is comfort for all who have seen in Jesus of Nazareth the image of the invisible God. It is the consolation of all who have found in him the ultimate assurance that God is on our side. It is, above all, comfort to all who find it hard to bear the cross. It was not easy for the Master.

Luke has followed Mark's passion narrative but has notably changed the tone of it. The Lucan Jesus is never distraught or agitated. The Lucan Jesus never experiences Godforsakenness. Instead, he is serenely in communion with his Father throughout, to the very end: 'Father, into your hands I commend my spirit' (23:46). Here is a positive aspect of the passion not found in Mark. And, in the

Lucan gospel, it is not surprising to find stress on the healing and forgiving power of God mediated through Jesus, even in the passion. We turn to some special Lucan features in his passion narrative.[31]

Gethsemane (22:39-46)

Mark tells us that at Gethsemane 'Jesus began to be distressed and agitated' and he said to his disciples: 'I am deeply grieved even unto death' (14:33-34). In contrast, Luke has no portrait of Jesus in distress. The Lucan Jesus is so at peace with God that he cannot be distraught by suffering. There is, besides, a concern to have Jesus in his passion revealed as a model for Christian sufferers and martyrs. Proper to Luke are vv. 43-44 – 'Then an angel from heaven appeared to him and gave him strength. And being in agony, he prayed more earnestly, and his sweat became like great drops of blood falling down on the ground.' Assisting angels figure in stories of martyrs, Jewish and Christian. On a wider showing, an angel can dramatise answer to prayer, as in the Tobit story. Luke's angel gives striking expression to Hebrews 5:7 – 'he was heard because of his reverent submission.' The agónia of Lk 22:44 is not the distress and agitation of Mk 14:33. Rather, it refers to anguished tension in face of entry into the peirasmos, the great trial (v. 40). It is an athletic metaphor; see 1 Tim 6:12; 2 Tim 4:7, 'fighting the good fight (agón).'

> The Father cannot spare Jesus from drinking the cup, but the strengthening angel prepares Jesus so that he arises from prayer in tense readiness for the combat with the approaching power of darkness (Lk 22:53). The sweat that breaks forth and flows as freely as blood is the visible sign of that readiness for the cup and hints at martyrdom.[32]

It should be acknowledged that the authenticity of these verses is not quite clear; the manuscript witness is almost equally divided for and against. On the whole, it is easier to explain omission rather than later insertion. Christian scribes would have been embarrassed by the portrait of a Jesus who needed angelic assistance.

Peter's Failure (22:47-62)

The question, 'Lord, should we strike with the sword?' (22:49) is a Lucan addition echoing the Last Supper reference to possession of two swords (v. 38). Distinctively Lucan is Jesus' healing of the servant whose ear had been severed (v. 51). It is an instance of a recurring motif: Jesus is healer and Saviour throughout the passion. Another Lucan touch is 'the power of darkness' (v. 53). At the close of the temptation story the devil departed from Jesus until 'an opportune time' (4:13). One is reminded of the fourth gospel and the presence of the devil in Judas (Jn 13:2, 27). The reference is, too, an echo of Satan's demand to sift Simon (Lk 22:31). 'The Lord turned and looked at Peter' (22:61). Only Luke has Jesus together with Peter in the house of the high priest. It is this turning of Jesus towards him and gazing upon him, rather than the cockcrow, that brings Peter to recall 'the word of the Lord' (see v. 34). It was in response to this gracious look that Peter 'went out and wept bitterly' (v. 62). Satan has well and truly sifted Peter (v. 31); Jesus displays his enduring care, already promised (22:32).

The Jewish Interrogation (22:66-71)

In Mk 14:55-59 the Sanhedrists summoned witnesses who, it was hoped, would help to convict Jesus of threatening to destroy the Temple. Luke does not have these witnesses at Jesus' interrogation, but the accusation surfaces in the Stephen trial: 'They set up false witnesses who said ... "we have heard him say that this Jesus of Nazareth will destroy this place and will change the customs that Moses handed on to us".' (Acts 6:13-14). Luke keeps the second part of his work in mind. In Mark the high priest, in view of unsatisfactory testimony, put, as a last resort, the challenging question directly to Jesus: 'Are you the Messiah, the Son of the Blessed One?' (Mk 14:61; see Mt 26:63). Here, Luke has separated the titles: 'If you are the Messiah, tell us'(22:67); 'Are you, then, the Son of God?' (v. 70). Luke is thereby suggesting a distinction between 'Messiah' as understood by Jews, and the Christian understanding of 'the Son of God.' The fourth gospel, also, has separate questions (Jn 10:24, 33-36) – a link between Lucan and Johannine traditions. Jesus' response to the Son of God title – 'You (yourselves) say that I am' (Lk 22:70) – is frequently taken to be an evasive answer, a qualified affirmation. In fact, it is a firm declaration. The Lucan Jesus has turned the question of the Jewish authorities into an affirmation of the highest Christian title. In between the questions Jesus had declared: 'But from now on the Son of Man will be seated at the right hand of the power of God' (v. 69).

Before Herod and Pilate (23:1-25)

Proper to Luke is Pilate's sending Jesus to Herod Antipas. What is at issue is a preliminary investigation *(anakrisis)*, a practice of Roman provincial officials. We find a similar situation in Acts 25 where the procurator Festus brought Paul before Agrippa. For Luke, the significance of the episode is that Herod emerges as an important witness to the innocence of Jesus – a point made explicitly by Pilate in 23:15. Early tradition had Herod hostile to Jesus (see 13:31). Here the same Herod 'treated him with contempt' in face of chief priests and scribes who stood 'vehemently accusing him' (23:10). He obviously did not set much store by their charges. Eminently Lucan is the observation: 'that same day Herod and Pilate became friends' (v. 12). This verse reflects Luke's theme of forgiveness and healing throughout the passion. Jesus was an occa-sion for the healing of the enmity of Pilate and Herod (v. 12).

Aside from Pilate's sending of Jesus to Herod, there are two other interesting features of Luke's Roman trial. In 23:2-5 there is marked conformity with trials of Paul in Acts. Compare Lk 23:2, 'We found this man perverting our nation, forbidding us to pay taxes to the emperor, and saying that he himself is the Messiah, a king' with Acts 24:1-2 where the high priest Ananias and elders accuse Paul to the governer Felix: 'We found this man ... an agitator among all the Jews throughout the world ... By examining him yourself you will be able to learn from him concerning everything of which we accuse him' (24:5, 8). In other words, in Lk 23:2, Luke is reflecting a Jew versus Christian polemic of the 70-80s.

The second factor shows one of the two major links (the other being Lk 22:67,70; Jn 10:24-25,33-36) with the Johannine tradition: Pilate's three 'not guilty' statements. These are: 'I find no basis for an accus-ation against this man' (Lk 23:4); 'You brought this man as one who was perverting the people; and here I have examined him in your presence and have not found this man guilty of any of your charges against him. Neither did Herod ... Indeed, he has done nothing to deserve death' (23:14-15); 'Why, what evil has he done? I have found in him no ground for the sentence of death' (23:22). No ambi-guity here. Compare Jn 18:38b; 19:4, 6. After these firm declarations of innocence, Pilate's abrupt capitulation is surprising in the story-line (Lk 23:23-25) – 'he handed over Jesus as they wished.' At this

point Mark (15:15) has Jesus flogged – a flogging being a preliminary part of execution by crucifixion. The Lucan Jesus never is
flogged or whipped. True, Pilate twice declared, 'I will therefore
have him chastised *(paideuein)* and then release him' (23:16, 22). The
chastisement is a whipping, not a severe flogging or scourging.
And, in Luke, it was not carried out.

To The Cross (23:26-31)

V. 26 reads literally, 'they put on him the cross to bring behind Jesus'.
The Lucan Simon of Cyrene is a positive figure. He smooths the
way to the description of others not opposed to Jesus. Luke has a
group of three parties favourable to Jesus before the crucifixion and
a comparable group after Jesus' death. This is a significant structur-
al modification of the Marcan narrative. *Before the crucifixion*
(23:26-32): Here we have Simon of Cyrene (v. 26), women who
bewailed Jesus (v. 27), two wrongdoers, one of whom will later proclaim the innocence of Jesus (v. 32). *After the death of Jesus* (23:47-49):
the centurion (v. 47), the crowds (v. 48) and the women (v. 49).
These respective triads are sympathetic to Jesus.

> These triads fit Luke's theological outlook that while some
> opposed Jesus ... the lives of many others were positively affected
> by the passion. If for Mark the passion manifests human failure
> and evil with the overcoming power of God manifested chiefly
> after Jesus dies, for Luke God's love, forgiveness and healing are
> already present throughout the passion.[33]

Luke has omitted the Marcan mockery of Jesus by the soldiers (Mk
15:16-20). Instead, after the reference to Simon of Cyrene he has
introduced a passage peculiar to himself (Lk 23:27-31).

The Daughters of Jerusalem (23:27-31)

These women who followed Jesus 'beating their breasts and wail-
ing for him' are surely sympathetic. Yet, his message to them is not
one of compassion; it is word of woe. In 13:34-35 Jesus had directly
addressed Jerusalem – the city that kills prophets and stones those
sent to it. He warned, 'Behold, your house is forsaken.' Here the
Daughters of Jerusalem represent the city; through them Jesus
addresses the inhabitants of Jerusalem. His threat refers to the
Roman destruction of the city when even innocent women and children would perish. The enigmatic sentence, 'For if they do this

when the wood is green, what will happen when it is dry?' (23:31) seems to mean that if the Jewish leaders and people treat Jesus thus in a time of peace how much the worse will *they* fare when the Romans wage war on them.

The oracle to the Daughters of Jerusalem as it stands reflects a wide-spread Christian interpretation of the Roman destruction of Jerusalem: they viewed it as divine judgment on those responsible for the death of God's Son, a punishment reaching to the next generation. It is the equivalent of Matthew's, 'His blood be on us and on our children!' (Mt 27:25). There is an unhappy human propensity to envisage an angry, even a vengeful, God. Luke is, however, less harsh than Matthew.

> The very fact that it is spoken to women who lament denies that the devastation will be deserved by all who live to see it. If the divine wrath cannot be diverted from Jerusalem because of its prolonged rejection of the prophets and Jesus, Luke shows that not all were hostile and leaves open the possibility that the God who had touched the hearts of Simon, and of the wrongdoers, and of the centurion, may in turn have been touched by the tears of those who lamented what was being done to Jesus. [34]

Father, Forgive Them (23:34-43)

Crucified between two criminals, at the place called The Skull, Jesus, with typical graciousness, prayed: 'Father, forgive them; for they do not know what they are doing' (23:34). The 'they' includes both the Romans who crucified Jesus and the Jews who had brought him to death. Jesus attributes ignorance to the obdurate chief priests and their allies. Luke is suggesting that even perpetrators of evil never really appreciate God's goodness or the strange wisdom of his purpose.

Like 22:43-44, this verse is textually unsure. Though omitted from important manuscripts it is present in equally weighty ones. The style is Lucan. And there is Stephen's parallel prayer, 'Lord, do not hold this sin against them' (Acts 7:20) – surely best understood as an echo of Jesus' prayer. All in all, it is much more reasonable to posit omission than to propose later insertion. In that case one must ask how a copyist may have come to omit this striking verse. Two reasons come to mind. It may have been judged too favourable to

Jews, and early Christians tended to regard Jews as relentless perse-
cutors. And there is the moral problem: how can there be forgiveness without genuine repentance? We have an unhappy penchant
for setting limits to divine forgiveness. Brown adverts to the irony
that the most beautiful sentence in the passion narrative should be
textually dubious and adds: 'Alas, too often not the absence of this
prayer from the text, but the failure to incorporate it into one's heart
has been the real problem.'[35]

While in Mark reaction to Jesus on the cross is wholly negative, in
Luke reaction is positive as well. His first observation is: 'And the
people stood by, watching' (23:35) – neutral bystanders. The 'people' in Mk 15:29 are the passersby who derided Jesus. In view of his
different estimation of 'the people' (Lk 23:35), Luke, who preserves
the series of three mockings of Mk 15:29-32, had to find another category of mockers. Thus, in Mark the mockers are passersby, chief
priests and scribes, and the co-crucified; in Luke they are the leaders, the soldiers, and one co-crucified. A challenge sounds through
the three Lucan mockeries: that Jesus should save himself. Jesus
will not save himself. Instead, he will grant salvation to another.

The episode of 23:40-43, salvation of a wrongdoer, relates to Luke's
theological purpose in two main regards: the 'other' wrongdoer
(kakourgos) is a further impartial witness to Jesus' innocence, and he
provides another instance of healing forgiveness during the passion. In rebuffing his co-sufferer, 'the other' acknowledges that both
of them had been condemned deservedly – 'but this man has done
nothing wrong'(23:41). He plays somewhat the same role as Pilate's
wife in Mt 27:19 who could affirm that a Jesus she had never met
was 'a just man'. The wrongdoer addressed Jesus, 'Jesus, remember
me when you come into your kingdom' (Lk 23:42). The direct
address, 'Jesus,' without qualification, is unique in the gospels. The
idea conveyed by 'into your kingdom' is that of Jesus ascending
into the kingdom from the cross. In dying, Jesus was passing
beyond time. The 'other' wrongdoer is asking to be remembered at
the moment of Jesus' vindication.

Typically, Jesus' response goes far beyond his expectation. 'Truly I
tell you, today you will be with me in Paradise' (23:43). 'Today'
means this very day; to be with Jesus in Paradise is to be with Christ
in the full presence of God. Some commentators have baulked at

this. A man who cannot have displayed *metanoia* (he had merely asked to be remembered) could not enjoy full salvation. In this view 'paradise' must mean some lesser form of closeness to God. Brown retorts tartly: 'A Jesus who was known as a friend of sinners (7:34), who received sinners and ate with them (15:2), may not have been squeamish about taking a sinner into the highest heaven once the sinner had asked to follow him.'[36] Jesus is, indeed, concluding the pattern of mercy shown throughout the passion narrative. 'Frequently called the episode of "the good thief," this is rather another aspect of the good Jesus.'[37]

Death and Burial (23:44-56)

There are a number of interesting Lucan features in his account of the death of Jesus. 'The curtain of the temple was torn in two' (39-45). In Mark the rending of the curtain or veil occurred after the death of Jesus (15:38). Luke has it between the darkness over the whole earth and Jesus' final words. The reason for the shift is that in 23:47-49 Luke has three types of people who respond compassionately and so affirm the saving import of the death. The ominous sign of the rending of the veil would not be in place in this context; it is more akin to the ominous darkness.

'Father, into your hands I commend my spirit' (23:46). Contrast with the dying cry in Mark recalls the Gethsemane situation. There Luke had omitted the Marcan description of a distraught and troubled Jesus; now he omits the Marcan Jesus' desperate cry of abandonment (Mk 15:34). The reason is theological: the Lucan Jesus is always wholly at peace with God. Similarly, in Mark, from the 'Abba' in Gethsemane (14:36) to the 'my God' on the cross (15:34) there is a movement of alienation. In contrast, the Lucan Jesus prays 'Father' on the Mount of Olives (22:42) and 'Father' at the end, on the cross (23:34). And his prayer on each occasion is peculiar to Luke.

We have noted that on the way to the cross there were three reactions: of Simon of Cyrene, of a large (sympathetic) crowd, and of women – the Daughters of Jerusalem. After the death the reactors are, similarly, an individual, the people, and women. Specifically, these are the centurion who, on the basis of what he witnessed, glorified God and declared: 'Certainly, this man was just' (23:47); all the crowd who, having seen what happened, went home beating their breasts (23:48); Jesus' acquaintances and the women who had followed him from Galilee, observing from a distance (23:49). The first and third reactions are adapted from Mark. The other is Lucan, reflecting his more favourable attitude towards the Jewish people.

The reaction of the centurion is noteworthy. In Mark his is the climactic statement of that gospel, a full Christain profession of faith: 'Truly this man was God's Son' (15:39). Luke's version rings so differently: 'Certainly this man was just' (23:47). Luke's concern is not that of Mark. His designation of Jesus as *dikaios* ('just') was meant to fit the pattern of repeated insistence on the fact that Jesus was not guilty of the charges levelled against him. The centurion had witnessed Jesus serenely accept death with a prayer of total confidence. This was no criminal! He can speak with conviction far beyond that of Pilate.

Of special interest here are Joseph of Arimathea and the women. Luke joins Mark (15:43) in having Joseph a member of the Sanhedrin – and not a disciple as in Matthew and John. Luke however specifies beyond Mark that Joseph 'had not agreed to the plan and action' of the other Sanhedrists (23:51). As one 'waiting expectantly for the kingdom of God' (v. 51) he takes his place with Zechariah, Elizabeth, Simeon, Anna. The women in this Lucan passage have a prominent role: they point to Easter and the discovery of the empty tomb. 'On the sabbath day they rested according to the commandment' (v. 56) – they are carefully law-observant. 'Thus at the end of the gospel the Lucan picture of the burial and resurrection of Jesus in Jerusalem features pious, law-observant characters of the same type as depicted at the beginning during Jesus' infancy and boyhood visits to Jerusalem (2:22-24, 25, 37, 41-42).'[38]

VINDICATION

The Riddle of the Tomb (24:1-12)

It is clear, from the New Testament, that Christians were, from the first, convinced that the crucified Jesus was not held by death. In Jewish faith and prayer, God is he who 'makes the dead live'. Jewish faith and hope looked to a resurrection of the righteous at the end of time. What the first Christians asserted was that, in the person of Jesus of Nazareth, this divine act had taken place. Jewish expectation was eschatological: resurrection was an event of the end-time. Christians asserted that an eschatological event had taken place in time. If one can put it so, the resurrection of Jesus is an event at once eschatological and historical. In essence it is a spiritual event, beyond our world of time, and it has impinged on our world of time.

The passage Lk 24:1-12 (based on Mk 16:1-8) breaks fresh ground. Luke explicitly records failure to find the body of Jesus. The women (v. 10) had come, as in Mark, to anoint the body. While they puzzled over the absence of the body of 'the Lord Jesus' (v. 3), 'two men in dazzling clothes stood by them' (v. 4) – a fascinating development of Mark's 'young man' and Matthew's 'angel of the Lord' (Mt 28:2). The 'two men' challenge the women's concern with the tomb: why are you seeking the living one in this place of the dead? (v. 5). In vv. 6-8 we have a striking example of Luke's editorial freedom. Since, in his theological plan, the climax of his gospel must be in Jerusalem he cannot, without bringing about an anticlimax, record apparitions in Galilee. So he rewrote Mark 16:7 and changed the promise of an appearance in Galilee into a prophecy made by Jesus 'while he was still in Galilee'. Again, unlike the women in Mark 'who said nothing to anyone' (Mk 16:8), the women in Luke 'told all this to the eleven and to all the rest' (Lk 24:9). The 'apostles', however, set no store by this 'idle tale' (v. 11). V. 12 offers one of the contacts with the Johannine tradition in Luke's passion and resurrection narrative. It tells that Peter went hastily to the tomb, saw the linen cloths (which had wrapped the body of Jesus) lying there, and came away, quite puzzled.

The Road To Emmaus (24:13-35)

This charming story is proper to Luke. It is more than story – it is a sophisticated eucharistic catechesis: a 'liturgy of the word' followed by a 'liturgy of the eucharist'. The conversation between Jesus and the two disciples, in which they discuss recent events and he answers them, is a clear outline of the early preaching in Acts. Jesus lived, died, and was raised from the dead, a fact which is witnessed in the scriptures and supported by the testimony of the apostles.

The description of the situation of the two disciples is poignant. They had been impressed by Jesus the man; they had hoped for a divine intervention while he was alive; their hope had been shattered by his death. They had obviously remained firmly tied to a Jewish expectation of the Messiah. After Jesus had explained what the scriptures really taught about the coming Messiah, they gained a deeper insight into the revelation of God in Christ. In the plan of God the cross was the necessary road to glory: 'Was it not necessary that the Messiah should suffer these things and then enter into his glory?' (24:26). There is a lot of ourselves in those two disciples. The ragged story of our life reveals its full splendour only when viewed in the context of Christ.

But the disciples did not really recognise Jesus until 'the breaking of the bread' (24:31, 35). Luke's readers could not have missed the point. Not only was 'the breaking of the bread' already a familiar designation of the eucharist, the terms describing the actions of Jesus at table – he took ... blessed ... broke ... gave (v. 30) – are explicitly eucharistic language (see 22:19). Luke is telling us here that in the eucharist we experience a meeting with Christ. We share a meal with Jesus in which he gives himself to us. The risen Jesus is met when and whenever the church 'breaks bread'.

He Opened Their Minds (24:36-52)

The appearance story (24:36-43) has quite obvious apologetic motifs: Jesus shows that he is the same person whom the disciples had known prior to the crucifixion by pointing to his body and by eating before them. As in all appearance stories the risen Jesus is not immediately recognisable (v. 37); a gesture or word is necessary before the disciples recognise the Lord. This is quite a clever way of making the point that resurrection is not a return to earthly life; Jesus has risen to a new life beyond death. He is the same person – yet transformed. Here the point is firmly made that the risen Jesus is no 'ghost'. The assertion that he invited touching of his (wounded) hands and feet and that he ate in their presence is, in the apologetic of the time, a firm Christian rejection of any challenge to the reality of the new life of their Lord.

At the close of his gospel (24:44-49), Luke summarises the final commission of Jesus to his disciples; this he repeats at the beginning of Acts (1:3-8). More pointedly, the outline and words of this gospel passage echo the apostolic *kerygma* of Acts. Jesus first (v. 44) recalls

the occasions on which he had warned the disciples that he, in fulfilment of the will of God enshrined in the scriptures, would have to
suffer, die, and rise again (see 9:22, 44; 17:25; 18:31-33; 22:37). 'While
I was still with you' (v. 44): Jesus has entered into his glory (v. 26) by
his exaltation to the Father (Jn 20:17); his relations with the disciples
are not what they were before the glorification.

Then (vv. 45-48) he gave them a new understanding of the Old
Testament (vv. 45-48), an insight that will enable them to see how
and where it 'bears witness to him' (see Jn 5:39). Reinterpretation of
the Old Testament is a basic element of the early kerygma: the
dawning of the age of fulfilment (v. 44; see Acts 2:16; 3:18,24); the
suffering of the Messiah and his resurrection on the third day (v. 46;
see Acts 2:23-24; 3:13-15; 4:10). The kerygma always includes the
proclamation of repentance and forgivenesss of sins, a proclamation to humankind – the universalist note is very much at home in
Luke (Acts 2:38- 39; 3:19-20; 4:12). These are the points which Paul
developed in his discourse at Antioch of Pisidia (Acts 3:26-41). The
message of salvation will go forth from Jerusalem, preached by the
apostles who are witnesses of the fulfilment of the prophecies (see
Acts 1:8), men who had seen the risen Christ and can attest that this
Lord is the same Jesus with whom they had lived (Acts 1:21; 2:32;
3:15; 5:32; 10:39-42; 13:31). The disciples are convincing witnesses
and efficacious missionaries because they have seen the Lord and
have believed in him. All who would, effectively, bear witness to
Christ must have encountered him in personal and living faith.
Today, when the call of the apostolate is urgent and the role of witness is seen as the obligation of every Christian, we are more keenly
aware that religion is not the acceptance of a body of doctrine nor
the adherence to a code of law, but attachment to a person.
Knowledge of Christ Jesus, in the biblical sense of acceptance and
commitment, is the essence of Christian life. It is obviously the first
requirement of an apostle.

Luke has undoubtedly given the impression that all the events of
chapter 24 had taken place on Easter day (see vv. 1, 13, 22, 29, 44,
50). This arrangement is editorial and the passage vv. 44-53 is a tele-
scoped version of Acts 1:3-14. Jesus did ascend to his Father on
Easter day (Jn 20:17) – or, from the cross (Lk 23:43). It is clear that
the Ascension in question here is the same as that in Acts – the final,

visible departure of the risen Jesus forty days (Acts 1:3) after the resurrection. 'As far as Bethany' (v. 50): in Acts the place of ascension is 'the mount called Olivet' (Acts 1:12) – Bethany lies on the eastern slope of the Mount of Olives. With hands raised in blessing (see Lev 9:22; Sir 50:22) Jesus parted from them (Acts 1:9). The joy of the disciples (vv. 52) at the moment of parting, though at first sight surprising, is explained by their realisation that 'the Lord is risen indeed' (v. 34). And they have his assurance that, very soon, they will be 'clothed with power from on high' (v. 49). Their minds have been opened to understand the scriptures: now they have grasped the plan of God and they realise that Christ, their Lord, has triumphed. Thankfully, they hasten to glorify God in his temple. Luke has closed his gospel as he began it, in the Temple; yet all is changed, changed utterly! He has shown the 'time of Israel' yielding to the 'time of Christ.' And now, about to begin his account of the word of salvation going forth from Jerusalem to 'the end of the earth' (Acts 1:8), he leaves us at the beginning of a new age, the 'time of the church.'

CONCLUSION

While Luke's passion narrative is based on Mark's version, it differs from Mark in structure and tone. Luke has some affinity with the Johannine tradition. Indeed, one might say that Luke's portrait of Jesus is halfway between the passion pictures of Mark and John. His Jesus is not the anguished man of Mark's Gethsemane and cross. Nor is he yet the majestic Jesus who dominates the Johannine story. Luke's Jesus, though rejected and mocked and suffering, is ever in serene communion with the Father. He does not experience Godforsakenness. His death is not with a lonely cry but with a tranquil prayer, 'Father, into your hands I commend my spirit.' It is not chance that this prayer finds an echo in Stephen's death vision: 'I see the heavens opened and the Son of Man standing at the right hand of God!' (7:56).

In Luke the disciples fare better than in Mark. Luke has no blunt, 'All of them deserted him and fled' (Mk 14:50), at the arrest of Jesus; they simply disappear from his story. If Peter does linger to deny his Lord, he experiences the look, surely full of tender understanding, of Jesus. And he will recall the comforting assurance, 'I have prayed for you' (22:31). The Jewish participants are shown in a less negative light. A multitude of people follow Jesus to Calvary, do not join in mocking him and, after his death, go home beating their breasts in a gesture of mourning. The Daughters of Jerusalem bewail him.

Perhaps the most distinctive, surely the most comforting, theme of Luke's passion narrative is his portrayal of the healing and forgiving power of God flowing from Jesus throughout the passion. Jesus healed the wound of one of those come to arrest him. He healed the enmity that had existed between his judges (Pilate and Herod). He looked upon a fallen Peter with deep compassion. He prayed forgiveness on those who brought about his death, acknowledging that they did not really know what they had done. He promised to take with him into the presence of the Father a wrongdoer who simply asked to be remembered by him. In all of this Jesus is manifestly the Jesus who walks through the pages of Luke. But never more than in the passion is Luke, in Dante's phrase, *scriba mansuetudinis Christi* – chronicler of God's foolish love manifest in Jesus. We need Mark's story to remind us of the awfulness of the deed and to urge us to come to terms with the reality of the cross. We need Luke's gentler story to discern the forgiving love of God shine through the worst that humankind can wreak.

The predictions of the passion had ended with the assurance: 'on the third day be raised' (Lk 9:22; 18:33). Death could not be, and was not, the end. Luke makes his point in Acts, in Peter's inaugural address to his fellow Jews:

> This man, handed over to you according to the definite plan and foreknowledge of God, you crucified and killed by the hands of those outside the law. But God raised him up, having freed him from death, because it was impossible for him to be held in its power (Acts 2:23-24).

God has the first word, and the last. Luke's message is that God's definitive word is word of salvation.

Conclusion

From the first, Luke has struck a distinctive note. His infancy narrative (Lk 1-2) is christologically provocative. Jesus was, wholly, one of us; yet, there was something special about his becoming and his birth. Luke has followed through the principle: the child is father of the man. The Jesus he, indirectly, presents in his infancy narrative is, recognisably, the Jesus whom he advanced throughout his gospel. Jesus is prophet and teacher, God's spokesperson. Schooled by his Baptist mentor, he would, at first, have had something of John's Amos-like fervour. Happily, he soon found his own line. He became prophet of God's unconditional love – and paid the price. Jesus had empathy with the world of his day. Though he himself was not poor, he was keenly aware of the misery of the destitute. He displayed a respect, a reverence, for women.

To appreciate Luke's overall purpose, his second work (Acts) must be taken into consideration. Then one can see that his object was to present the definitive phase of God's saving intervention, from the birth of the Baptist to the proclaiming of the gospel in the capital of the Gentile world. His theme is the progress of the good news from Jerusalem to Rome; it is above all a message of salvation to the Gentiles. Simeon had seen in Christ 'a light for revelation to the Gentiles' (Lk 2:32), and Paul's closing words to the Roman Jews are: 'Let it be known to you then that this salvation of God has been sent to the Gentiles; they will listen' (Acts 28:28). All of this follows, in the plan of God, on Christ's rejection by Israel, for that rejection led to his death and exaltation and to the promise of universal salvation. 'Thus it is written that the Messiah is to suffer and to rise from the dead on the third day, and that repentance and forgiveness of sins is to be proclaimed in his name to all nations beginning from Jerusalem' (Lk 24:46-47). It is indeed a constant (theological) preocupation of the evangelist to centre his gospel around Jerusalem, because Jeruasalem is for him the holy city of God and the theatre of the great redemptive event, the passion and triumph of Christ. In Jerusalem the gospel begins (1:5) and in Jerusalem it closes (24:52-53).

Luke has a gentle soul. It is because of this that he has discerned the tenderness of Jesus. It is characteristic of him that he has omitted the cursing of the fig tree (Mk 11:12-14; Mt 21:18-19) and has given instead the parable of the Barren Fig Tree (Lk 13:6-9) – 'let it alone for one more year'. In the same vein he has assembled the three parables of chapter 15: the Lost Sheep, the Lost Coin, the Lost Boy. We, too, must have something of the mercy of a forgiving God, and the father's gentle rebuke to the sulking elder son has a message for all of us: 'We had to celebrate and rejoice, because this brother of yours was dead and has come to life; he was lost and has been found' (15:32).

Perhaps nowhere more than in the moving passage on the 'woman of the city who was a sinner' (7:36-50) do we see Jesus as Luke saw him. The Lord did not hesitate between the self-righteous Pharisee and the sinner, and his words were clear and to the point: 'Therefore, I tell you, her sins, which were many, have been forgiven; hence she has shown great love' (7:47). Luke alone records the words of Jesus to the 'good thief' (23:43) and his prayer for those who engineered his death: 'Father, forgive them; for they do not know what they are doing' (23:34). He alone tells of the look that moved Peter so deeply (22:61). Everywhere, at all times, there is forgiveness. It has been well said that the gospel of Luke is the gospel of great pardons.

Notes

1. Harrington, Wilfrid J., *Mark: Realistic Theologian* (Dublin: The Columba Press, 1996).
2. Johnson, Luke T., *The Gospel of Luke*. A Michael Glazier Book. (Collegeville,MN: Liturgical Press, 1991), 3.
3. Kingsbury, Jack Dean, 'The Plot of Luke's Story of Jesus,' *Interpretation* (1994). 376; see 369-378.
4. The verb *dei*, 'it is necessary' – like the verb *paradidómi*, 'to deliver up' – occurs freely in the gospels and Acts. The meaning is brought out in Acts 2:23, in Peter's first speech to Israel: 'This man [Jesus], handed over to you according to the definite plan and foreknowledge of God, you crucified and killed by the hands of those outside the law.' This surely does not point to a calculated, inflexible divine purpose. Rather, it is an attempt to come to terms with the inexplicable fact of the death of Jesus. It is acceptance of mystery: we cannot perceive the reason, but, God knows .
5. This firm declaration of the Lucan Jesus is, assuredly, a programme of radical liberation – rightly discerned by liberation theologians. Noteworthy is the fact that the quotation from Isaiah stops short of the phrase 'and the day of vengeance of our God' (Is 61:2). The God of Luke, prodigal Father of the 'friend of sinners,' is wholly in the business of salvation.
6. Advertance to women remains a notable feature even when it is seen that Luke's stance is not quite as positive as it looks at first sight. See pp. 70-72.
7. Schneiders, Sandra M., *The Revelatory Text. Interpreting the New Testament as Sacred Scripture* (San Francisco: Harper, 1991), 107-108.
8. Meier, John P., *A Marginal Jew. Vol. I. Rethinking the Historical Jesus* (New York: Doubleday, 1991).
9. Murphy-O'Connor, Jerome, 'John the Baptist and Jesus: History and Hypotheses,' *New Testament Studies* 36 (1990), 359-374.

10. The title of this chapter is, already, acknowledgment of my indebtedness to the scholarship of Raymond E. Brown: *The Birth of the Messiah*. New Updated Edition (New York: Doubleday, 1993).

11. Johnson, L. T., op. cit., 39.

12. Quirinius was legate of Syria 6-7 AD. In 6 AD he took a census of Judaea, Samaria and Idumaea, but not of Galilee, territory of Herod Antipas. Jesus was born before the death of Herod the Great in 4 BC.

13. Johnson, L. T., op. cit., 53.

14. Johnson, L. T., op. cit., 61.

15. Harrington, W., op. cit., 30-72.

16. Danker, F. W., *Jesus and the New Age: A Commentary on St Luke's Gospel* (Philadelphia: Fortress, 1988), 110.

17. Harrington, W., op. cit., 73-84.

18. Betz, Hans Dieter, *The Sermon on the Mount. Hermeneia* (Minneapolis: Fortress, 1995).

19. See p. 70-72.

20. See above. p. 43-45.

21. Seim,Turid Karlsen, *The Double Message. Patterns of Gender in Luke-Acts* (Edinburgh: T. & T. Clark, 1994), 162. See 25-163. Relevant is a telling comment of Edward Schillebeeckx: 'If I understand them correctly, what the feminist theologians have done is to trace and discover the fundamental error in Western theology since Augustine especially. The sin of pride, which is, of course, the principal sin, has always been seen as a sinful preoccupation with self-assertion. This has made us blind to the fact that the female preoccupation with self-denial was imposed on women by consciously and unconsciously living in the sexist patriarchal structures of society and the Church. Those structures forced women to deny themselves in the name of what was in fact an un-Christian understanding both of pride and of self-sacrifice. The dominant Church doctrine of sin and grace encouraged women to be passive and to deny themselves. Now the feminist theologians have come to understand that an authentic doctrine of sin and grace must include the idea of responsible self-assertion on the part of women with and for others, an idea that, if made a reality, is liberating.' *God Is New Each Moment* (New York: Seabury Press, 1983), 73.

22. Harrington, Wilfrid, *Jesus and Paul. Signs of Contradiction* (Wilmington, DE: M. Glazier, 1987), 57-61, 148-162.

23. Seim, T.K., op. cit., 260.

24. E.P. Sanders has studied, in detail, the meaning of 'sinners' in the Judaism of Jesus' day. See *Jesus and Judaism* (London: SCM, 1985), 174-211. The brief sketch here leans heavily on his later treatment of the subject in *The Historical Figure of Jesus* (London: Penguin Books, 1995), 226-237.

25. 'Jesus was aware that he was acting as God would do. He translates God's action for men and women. The parables tell of the one lost sheep, a lost coin, a lost son. To fellow-Jews who were irritated at his dealings with impure people Jesus wants to make clear through his action that God turns to vulnerable men and women: Jesus acts as God acts. So he embodies a claim that in his actions and works God himself is present. To act as Jesus does is praxis of the kingdom of God and also shows what the kingdom of God is: salvation for men and women.' Edward Schillebeeckx, *Jesus in Our Western Culture* (London: SCM, 1987), 20.

26. Sanders, E.P., *The Historical Figure of Jesus*, 234.

27. Sanders, E.P., op. cit., 231.

28. Sanders, E.P., op. cit., 236-237.

29. 'Zacchaeus offered a lot more than the law require: that a person who defrauds another should repay him, add 20% as a fine, and then sacrifice a lamb as a guilt offering (Lev 6:1-7).' E.P. Sanders, op. cit., 230.

30. See Sanders, E.P., *Jesus and Judaism*, 174-211; Harrington, W., *God Does Care* (Dublin: The Columba Press, 1994), 53-68.

31. I am beholden to the major study of Raymond E. Brown, *The Death of the Messiah* (New York/London: Doubleday/Chapman, 1994). This two-volume work of 1608 pages is not only the most thorough, it is far and away the best modern scholarly analysis of the gospel passion narratives. See W. Harrington, *The Gracious Word, Year C* (Dublin: Dominican Publications, 1997), 66-80. Our treatment of Luke's passion narrative has frequent reference to Mark's parallel text: See W. Harrington, *Mark: Realistic Theologian* (Dublin: The Columba Press, 1996), 123-137.

32. Brown, R.E., op. cit., 190.

33. Brown, R.E., op. cit., 931.

34. Brown, R.E., op. cit., 931-932.

35. Op. cit., 980.
36. Op. cit., 1010.
37. Brown, R.E., op. cit., 1013.
38. Brown, R.E., op. cit., 1287.

For Reference and Further Study

LUKE

G. B. Caird, *St Luke* (London: Penguin Books, 1963).

F. W. Danker, *Jesus and the New Age. A Commentary on St Luke's Gospel* (Philadelphia: Fortress, 1988).

L. Doohan, *Luke. The Perennial Spirituality* (Santa Fe: Bear, 1985).

J. A. Fitzmyer, *The Gospel According to Luke.* 2 vols. (New York: Doubleday, 1981, 1985).

L. T. Johnson, *Luke.* Sacra Pagina 3. A Michael Glazier Book (Collegeville, MN: Liturgical Press, 1993).

R. Karris, *What Are They Saying about Luke and Acts?* (New York: Paulist, 1979).

E. LaVerdiere, *Luke.* New Testament Message 5 (Wilmington, DE: M. Glazier, 1980).

M. Prior, *Jesus the Liberator.* (Sheffield: Academic Press, 1995).

Interpretation (1994). *The Gospel of Luke.*

GENERAL

R. E. Brown, *The Birth of the Messiah.* Updated Edition (New York: Doubleday, 1993).

— *The Death of the Messiah.* 2 vols. (New York/London: Doubleday/ Chapman, 1994).

L. T. Johnson, *Acts of the Apostles.* Sacra Pagina 5. A Michael Glazier Book. (Collegeville, MN: Liturgical Press, 1992).

J. P. Meier, *A Marginal Jew. Vol. 1. Rethinking the Historical Jesus.* (New York: Doubleday, 1991).

E. P. Sanders, *Jesus and Judaism.* (London: SCM, 1985).

— *The Historical Figure of Jesus.* (London: Penguin Books, 1995).

T. K. Seim, *The Double Message. Patterns of Gender in Luke-Acts.* (Edinburgh: T. & T. Clark, 1994).

Index to Lucan Passages